CREOLE

FOR THE

SOUL

Creole for the Soul

Published by Our Lady Queen of Heaven School

Copyright © 2009 by Our Lady Queen of Heaven School
3908 Creole Street
Lake Charles, Louisiana 70605
Phone: 337-477-7349
Fax: 337-477-7384

Art © Felix Falgoust

This cookbook is a collection of favorite recipes, which are
not necessarily original recipes.

ISBN: 978-0-615-19745-6

Edited, Designed, and Produced by

CommunityClassics™

an imprint of

FRP.

a wholly owned subsidiary of Southwestern/Great American, Inc.
P. O. Box 305142
Nashville, Tennessee 37230
800-358-0560

Manufactured in China

First Printing: 2009

3,000 copies

SPECIAL ACKNOWLEDGMENTS

CREOLE FOR THE SOUL COMMITTEE

Annabelle Byrnes-Bartell
Tracy Cunningham
Julie Flaherty
Ginny Henning

This book is dedicated to…

Our beautiful and talented students, who are the future.
We do it all for them!

And Jesus said, "Suffer little children and forbid them not,
to come unto me: for such is the kingdom of heaven."

Matthew 19:14 (KJV)

A special thank-you to…

OLQH SCHOOL ADMINISTRATION, FACULTY, AND STAFF

Mrs. Mary Anne Hipp, Principal
Mr. James Newman, Assistant Principal
Mrs. Lisa Jakel, Public Relations Director
Faculty and Staff of OLQH School,
for their patient and wonderful support.

Special Consultant

Dawn Harrington, of the Harrington Gallery,
Sulphur, Louisiana, who was a huge part of the creative process

"I am not afraid of tomorrow; I have seen yesterday; and I love today."

—WILLIAM ALLEN WHITE

TABLE OF CONTENTS

ABOUT THE ARTIST

Felix Falgoust

Felix Falgoust is a native of Sulphur, Louisiana, who is quickly making a name for himself as an artist. He is a senior mechanical design engineer for local industries, as well as a full-time artist. Among his many contributions to the art of Louisiana…

- *marketed seven prints from gouache paintings of indigenous animal characters in assorted Louisiana settings entitled the La Bonne Vie Series;*
- *a collection of pen and ink drawings of local historical events for the City of Lake Charles;*
- *a banner design for the Lake Charles Tourist Bureau;*
- *design artist for the seventeenth annual Tamale Fiesta poster in Zwolle, Louisiana;*
- *designs for two of the "Gators on the Geaux" featured in Lake Charles as "Senator Gator," sponsored by Senator Willie Mount, and "Ubiquitous Swamp King," sponsored by the music department at McNeese State University, which were part of a fund-raising effort by the Lake Charles Symphony;*
- *cover illustration designs for the area Dining Guide;*
- *illustrator for Lagniappe Magazine, featured in "Weird News," "Cajun Humor," and "File 13";*
- *known for his caricatures of local politicians and community leaders;*
- *credited with designing logos and illustrating brochures, cards, and invitations for ad agencies;*
- *received commissions for various portraits done in media ranging from pastels and acrylics to bronze and marble;*
- *designed the stage for the 2001 Gridiron Show, a variety show staged by the Ad and Press Club designed to fund scholarships.*

When he isn't working, Felix enjoys spending time with his thirteen-year-old daughter, Julia, who is a very talented young lady and an inspiration to her father.

OLQH School is honored to feature Felix Falgoust's wonderful, whimsical art in its cookbook, *Creole for the Soul.*

FOREWORD

Chef John D. Folse

Ahhh! A little taste of heaven! And it's about time, too. Our Lady Queen of Heaven School has been delightfully perched on Creole Street in Lake Charles since it was dedicated in 1958. I cannot think of a better way to mark a golden anniversary than with *Creole for the Soul*, a wonderful memoir of recipes from the family and friends of Our Lady Queen of Heaven parish.

History is recorded on the pages of cookbooks. Every recipe is a snapshot of life during a certain era. I am certain this cookbook will leave an indelible, and delectable, impression on the palates of its many patrons.

I have had the distinct honor, privilege, and pleasure of creating wonderful cocktail receptions, soirees, and luncheons for the patrons, parents, and personnel of Our Lady Queen of Heaven School on numerous occasions. I have never failed to be impressed with the dedication to quality education exhibited at Our Lady Queen of Heaven. It is obvious that professionals are in the classrooms and halls, that parents are involved in the students' activities and homework, and that the pupils themselves are intellectually, culturally, and spiritually nourished every day toward success in academic excellence.

Congratulations on a wonderful cookbook. I know that a legacy of great recipes is recorded on the pages of *Creole for the Soul*. Certainly, the gastronomes of today and the budding culinarians and epicureans of tomorrow will savor every page.

God bless,

Chef John D. Folse

HISTORY OF OUR LADY QUEEN OF HEAVEN CATHOLIC SCHOOL

Our Lady Queen of Heaven Catholic School was established and opened on October 12, 1958, under the direction of the Reverend Adrian Van Hal, pastor of Our Lady Queen of Heaven ("OLQH") Parish in Lake Charles, Louisiana. The school began with twenty-four students in kindergarten, with the class being held in the Knights of Columbus building. It grew through the years, adding grades, classrooms, students, and faculty, until it became the current school of approximately 753 students, attending in grades pre-K through eighth, with an Early Childhood Center.

The school's principals through the years have been the following: Sister Elaine Schaeffler, S.S.N.D., principal 1963; Sister Paulette Strakos, S.S.N.D., principal 1969; Sister Gloria Cain, S.S.N.D., principal 1973; Elizabeth Niekamp, principal 1983; Jennifer Bellon, assistant principal 1993; Keith Bartlett, principal 1990; Mary Ann Moses, principal 1993; Mary Anne Hipp, principal 1998 to present; and James Newman, assistant principal 2003 to present.

Currently, the school houses three sections of grades pre-K through eighth, including one self-contained special education class. The Early Childhood Center has an enrollment of fifty-seven from ages six weeks to four years. The faculty consists of thirty-one classroom teachers, a full-time assistant principal, a guidance counselor, a director of religious education, a director of technology and telecommunications, a technology coach, a librarian, two physical education teachers, one part-time vocal music teacher, one instrumental music teacher, a kindergarten aide, a pre-kindergarten aide, a special education aide, a physical education aide, and two full-time and twelve part-time staff members at the Early Childhood Center.

The proceeds from the sale of *Creole for the Soul* will be used to make needed repairs and improvements to the school's gymnasium, which was originally the very first OLQH Church. The groundbreaking ceremony for the building was held on October 1, 1957. The building became the school's gymnasium in 1971 and remains a very vital part of our school activities today. Restoring the cornerstone building of what was the birth of Our Lady Queen of Heaven is the school's heartfelt wish for this huge endeavor.

❧ TO TEACH IS TO TOUCH THE FUTURE. ❧

Congratulations on Fifty Years of Excellence!

Breakfast

Cooking Up Fun With Kids

SECRET BUBBLE RECIPE

1 gallon water
½ cup clear or light-colored concentrated dishwashing liquid
¼ cup glycerine

Combine the water, dishwashing liquid and glycerine in a large
container and mix gently. The solution gets better with age.
The longer it stands, the stronger the bubbles.

**NOTE: *Glycerine may be purchased from your local
drugstore or pharmacy.***

Atchafalaya Apple Beignets

2 cups all-purpose flour
1 tablespoon baking powder
1/4 cup granulated sugar
1 teaspoon salt
1/4 teaspoon ground allspice
1 (750-milliliter) bottle sparkling wine
1 cup Calvados or sweet cider
1 1/4 cups granulated sugar
3 tart apples, peeled and cut into 1/4-inch rounds
Vegetable oil for frying
1/2 cup all-purpose flour
Confectioners' sugar to taste

Whisk 2 cups flour, the baking powder, 1/4 cup granulated sugar, the salt and allspice in a mixing bowl. Whisk in the sparkling wine gradually. The batter may be thin at first, but will thicken upon standing. Chill, covered, for 1 to 4 hours.

Mix the Calvados and 1 1/4 cups granulated sugar in a bowl. Submerge the apples in the mixture. Soak for 30 minutes; drain. Heat 3/4 inch oil to 350 degrees in a medium saucepan. Sift 1/2 cup flour into a shallow dish. Dust each apple round with the flour and dip in the batter to coat. Place carefully in the hot oil. The apple rounds will sink at first and then float to the top. Fry until golden brown. Remove to paper towels to drain. Sprinkle with confectioners' sugar.

Serves 15 to 20

*No one has yet fully realized the wealth of sympathy, kindness,
and generosity hidden in the soul of a child. The effort of every true education
should be to unlock that treasure.*

—EMMA GOLDMAN

"Honey Chile" Pancakes

Pecan Honey Butter

1/2 cup (1 stick) butter, softened
1/3 cup pecans, toasted and finely chopped
2 tablespoons local honey
1/8 to 1/4 teaspoon cinnamon

Pancakes

1 cup all-purpose flour
1 teaspoon baking powder
1/2 teaspoon baking soda
1/4 teaspoon salt
1 egg, lightly beaten
1 cup buttermilk
2 tablespoons local honey

To prepare the butter, combine the butter, pecans, honey and cinnamon in a bowl and mix well. Chill, covered, until serving time.

To prepare the pancakes, mix the flour, baking powder, baking soda and salt in a medium bowl. Add the egg, buttermilk and honey and mix well. Pour 1/4 cup of the batter onto a hot lightly greased griddle or in a skillet. Cook for 1 to 2 minutes or until bubbles appear on the surface and the underside is golden brown. Turn the pancake and cook until golden brown. Repeat with the remaining batter. Top each pancake with the butter.

Serves 13

She's a light eater; as soon as it is light, she starts eating.

—ANONYMOUS

Mascarpone French Toast Pirogues Floating in Warm Maple Syrup with Brandied Strawberries

Brandied Strawberries

4 teaspoons fruit brandy of choice,
　　such as Calvados

1/3 cup fresh orange juice

2 cups sliced fresh strawberries

Mascarpone Cheese

4 ounces cream cheese, softened

1 teaspoon butter, softened

2 tablespoons whipping cream

1 tablespoon sugar

1 teaspoon fresh lemon juice

1/2 teaspoon vanilla extract

Pirogues

8 miniature dry croissants

2 eggs

1/2 cup milk

1/2 teaspoon vanilla extract

1/8 teaspoon salt

Unsalted butter for frying

Warm maple syrup to taste

To prepare the strawberries, blend the brandy and orange juice in a glass measure. Pour over the strawberries in a bowl. Chill in the refrigerator for 2 to 6 hours.

To prepare the mascarpone cheese, beat the cream cheese and 1 teaspoon butter in a mixing bowl until creamy. Add the cream, sugar, lemon juice and 1/2 teaspoon vanilla and mix well.

To prepare the pirogues, slice the croissants into halves lengthwise. Spread 1 tablespoon of the mascarpone cheese on each of one-half of the croissant halves, leaving a 1/4-inch border. Top with the remaining croissant halves. Whisk the eggs, milk, 1/2 teaspoon vanilla and salt in a bowl. Pour into a baking dish. Melt unsalted butter in a large skillet over medium heat; do not brown. Place four of the pirogues in the batter and let stand for 4 to 6 seconds or until thoroughly coated. Turn and repeat the process on the other side. Carefully lift the pirogues from the batter, letting the excess batter drip back into the dish. Cook in the melted butter for 2 minutes or until brown, adding additional butter if needed. Turn and cook for 1 to 2 minutes or until brown. Remove the pirogues from the skillet with a clean spatula. Repeat with the remaining pirogues.

To serve, drain the brandied strawberries to remove the excess liquid. Place two pirogues on a serving plate. Top with maple syrup and the brandied strawberries.

Serves 4

He who walks in another's tracks leaves no footprints.

—JOAN L.

Gingerbread Waffles

2 cups sifted all-purpose flour
3/4 teaspoon baking soda
1/2 teaspoon salt
2 teaspoons ginger
2 egg whites, at room temperature
2 egg yolks
1 cup molasses
1/2 cup buttermilk
1/2 cup shortening, melted

Sift the flour, baking soda, salt and ginger together in a bowl. Beat the egg whites in a mixing bowl until soft peaks form. Beat the egg yolks in a mixing bowl until thick and pale yellow. Add the molasses, buttermilk and shortening and mix with a rotary beater. Add to the flour mixture and stir quickly just until moistened. Fold in the egg whites in eight to ten strokes. Cook in a waffle iron using the manufacturer's directions, cooking at a slightly lower temperature and for 1 to 2 minutes longer than regular waffles.

Serves 5

*You might be a Cajun if... You think the Fab Four are: John Folse,
Paul Prudhomme, Justin Wilson, and A. J. Smith.*

—ANONYMOUS

Bran Muffins with Southern-Style Preserved Figs

Preserved Figs
9 cups sugar
1 1/2 cups water
18 fresh figs
1 lemon, thinly sliced and seeded
1 orange, thinly sliced and seeded
6 cinnamon sticks
30 whole cloves
6 whole cardamom seeds

Muffins
1 cup sifted all-purpose flour
1 teaspoon baking powder
1/2 teaspoon salt
1/4 cup bran cereal
2/3 cup milk
1 teaspoon vanilla extract
1/2 cup shortening
3/4 cup sugar
1 egg

To prepare the figs, bring the sugar and water to a boil in a large saucepan. Reduce the heat to very low. Add the figs, lemon slices and orange slices. Tie the cinnamon sticks, cloves and cardamom in a cheesecloth bag. Add to the fig mixture. Simmer slowly for 1 hour or until the figs are glazed and the juice is syrupy and golden. Discard the spice bag. Carefully spoon the figs, lemon slices and orange slices into hot sterilized jars. Add the syrup, leaving 1/4 inch headspace; seal with two-piece lids. Process in a boiling water bath for 10 minutes.

To prepare the muffins, sift the flour, baking powder and salt together. Soak the cereal in the milk in a bowl. Stir in the vanilla. Cream the shortening and sugar in a mixing bowl until light and fluffy. Add the egg and beat well. Add the flour mixture alternately with the cereal mixture, beating constantly. Drop a teaspoonful of the batter into each greased muffin cup. Top each with a preserved fig. Fill each two-thirds full with the remaining batter. Bake at 375 degrees for 25 minutes.

Makes 1 1/2 dozen

A child is fed with milk and praise.
—MARY LAMB

Old Spanish Trail Granola Parfait

1/2 cup cold heavy cream	1 cup honey
1/4 cup confectioners' sugar	1 cup vegetable oil
2 cups milk	1 tablespoon cinnamon
1 teaspoon vanilla extract	1/2 cup (3 ounces) coarsely chopped
4 cups rolled oats	dried apricots
1/2 cup sunflower seeds	1 cup raisins
1/4 cup sesame seeds	2 nectarines, pitted and sliced
1/2 cup sliced almonds	1 cup sliced strawberries

Whisk the cream, confectioners' sugar, milk and vanilla in a large bowl until smooth.

Mix the oats, sunflower seeds, sesame seeds and almonds in a roasting pan. Combine the honey, oil and cinnamon in a bowl and mix well. Pour over the oat mixture and mix well. The mixture will be very dry. Bake at 350 degrees for 1 hour or until light golden brown, stirring at 20-minute intervals. Remove from the oven. Stir in the apricots and raisins. Let stand until cool.

Place a few slices of nectarines and strawberries in the bottom of four 1 3/4-cup parfait glasses or glass bowls. Divide one-half of the cream mixture among each of the glasses. Spoon about 1/4 cup granola over each serving. Add another layer of the remaining nectarines and strawberries. Add another layer of the remaining cream and top with the remaining granola. *(Note: This recipe is good with any combination of rolled oats, wheat, rye, rice or other rolled grain. Store a small quantity of the granola in a tightly sealed jar. Store the remaining granola in sealable freezer bags in the freezer until needed.)*

Serves 4

Kissing don't last; cookery do!

—GEORGE MEREDITH

Crepes with Honey Ham and Gruyère Cheese

3 eggs
1/2 cup water
1/2 cup all-purpose flour
3 tablespoons butter, melted
1/2 teaspoon salt

1/2 cup milk
Butter for brushing
Honey ham sandwich slices
Gruyère cheese

Process the eggs, water, flour, 3 tablespoons butter, salt and milk in a blender for 1 minute. Scrape down the side of the blender. Process for 30 seconds or until smooth. Chill for 1 hour.

Heat a seasoned crepe pan over medium-high heat until just hot enough for a drop of water to sizzle. Brush the crepe pan lightly with butter. Pour 2 to 4 tablespoons of the batter into the crepe pan at a time, tilting to coat the bottom. Cook until light brown on the bottom and dry on the top. Turn and brown the other side of the crepe if desired. Remove the crepe from the pan. Place the desired amount of ham and cheese in the middle of the warm crepe and fold the crepe over on each side. Let the crepe stand for a few minutes to allow the cheese to melt. Cool the pan slightly between cooking each crepe. Repeat with the remaining batter, ham and cheese. (Note: To freeze crepes, layer waxed paper, foil or plastic wrap between the crepes and place on a paper plate. Cover tightly with plastic wrap to seal out any moisture. Store in the freezer for several weeks. To thaw, place in the refrigerator for 8 to 10 hours, or unwrap the crepes and thaw in a 250-degree oven, carefully peeling the crepes apart as they thaw, or microwave on High for 1 to 2 minutes or until thawed.)

Serves 2

Confession of our faults is the next thing to innocence.
—Publius Syrus

Orleans Creamed Eggs

2 tablespoons butter
2 tablespoons all-purpose flour
1/2 teaspoon salt
1/4 teaspoon fresh cracked pepper
1 cup milk
1 teaspoon cognac
4 slices warm toast
Sliced white cheese of choice to taste
4 hard-cooked eggs, sliced
8 anchovy fillets (optional)

Melt the butter in the top of a double boiler. Stir in the flour, salt and pepper. Cook for 1 to 2 minutes or until smooth. Stir in the milk gradually. Cook until slightly thickened, stirring constantly. Stir in the cognac.

Arrange one slice warm toast on each serving plate. Layer cheese and one-fourth of the sliced eggs over the toast. Spoon the sauce over the top. Top each serving with two crisscrossed anchovy fillets.

Serves 4

Concentrate on finding your goal, then concentrate on reaching it.
—COLONEL MICHAEL FRIEDSMAN

Fabulous Crawfish Frittata with Leeks and Fresh Herbs

2 tablespoons unsalted butter
4 cups (12 ounces) thinly sliced leeks with tops
1 cup cooked crawfish tails, chopped
Salt and pepper to taste
6 eggs
1/2 cup mixture of fresh flat-leaf parsley,
     basil and mint, minced
1/4 cup (1 ounce) grated Parmesan cheese
Tabasco sauce to taste

Melt the butter in a 10-inch ovenproof skillet over medium heat until foamy. Add the leeks, crawfish, salt and pepper. Cook for 15 minutes or until the leeks are softened, stirring constantly. Reduce the heat to keep the leeks from browning.

Whisk the eggs in a bowl until blended. Whisk in the herbs, cheese, Tabasco sauce, salt and pepper. Add to the leek mixture, stirring to distribute evenly. Reduce the heat to low. Cook for 15 minutes or until the eggs are set around the edge, but still slightly moist in the center. Broil 6 inches from the heat source for 1 minute or until the top is puffed and golden brown and the center is firm. Remove the frittata carefully with a wide spatula to a cutting board. Cut into wedges and serve immediately.

Serves 4

Instead of giving myself reasons why I can't,
I give myself reasons why I can.

—ANONYMOUS

Breakfast Bruschetta with Crème Fraîche Eggs, Sweet Tomatoes and Bacon

1 cup heavy whipping cream
3 tablespoons buttermilk
6 slices French bread
2 tablespoons olive oil
6 slices bacon
1 cup assorted red, orange, yellow
    and green cherry tomatoes

Salt and freshly cracked pepper
    to taste
8 eggs
1/4 cup finely chopped fresh chives
3 tablespoons unsalted butter
Grated Parmesan cheese to taste
Extra-virgin olive oil for drizzling

Shake the whipping cream and buttermilk in a container with a lid. Let stand, covered, at room temperature for 12 to 24 hours or until thickened to the consistency of whipped cream. Chill until ready to use. Ultra-pasteurized cream tends to take longer to thicken. You may use 1/2 cup each sour cream and whipping cream to make the crème fraîche. Use the remaining crème fraîche with berries, on pancakes with fruit, or to make a delicious chocolate sauce. Crème fraîche may also be purchased prepared in select grocery stores.

Place the top oven rack in the position closest to the broiler. Brush both sides of each bread slice with olive oil. Place on a rimmed baking sheet. Place on the top oven rack and broil for 30 seconds or until the bread is toasted and the edges begin to brown slightly. Turn and broil for 30 seconds longer. Remove from the oven and cover with foil to keep warm.

Cook the bacon in a skillet until lightly crisp. Remove to paper towels to drain. Place the bacon under the foil next to the bread to keep warm. Cut the tomatoes into halves and place in a bowl. Sprinkle with salt and pepper and set aside.

Beat the eggs, 1/3 cup of the crème fraîche, the chives and salt to taste in a large bowl. Melt the butter in a large skillet over medium heat. Add the egg mixture. Cook for 1 minute; do not stir. Continue to cook for 1 to 2 minutes, gently turning over the egg mixture with a spatula to cook evenly; do not overcook.

To serve, place one slice toasted bread on each serving plate. Top with the eggs and the tomatoes. Crumble the bacon over the top. Sprinkle with Parmesan cheese. Drizzle with olive oil. Garnish with additional chives and serve. Voila!

Serves 6

Courage is grace under pressure.

—ERNEST HEMINGWAY

Bacon, Spinach and Brie Omelet

2 slices bacon
3/4 cup torn spinach
Salt and pepper to taste
3 eggs
1 tablespoon water
1 tablespoon unsalted butter
1 (1-inch) square Brie cheese with rind,
    cut into 1/8-inch-thick slices

Cook the bacon in a skillet over medium heat for 8 to 10 minutes or until crisp. Remove with a slotted spoon to paper towels to drain. Cool and crumble the bacon. Drain the skillet, leaving a thin film of the bacon drippings in the bottom of the skillet. Add the spinach and sauté for 45 seconds. Remove with tongs to a bowl and season with salt and pepper. Whisk the eggs, water, salt and pepper in a medium bowl until blended.

Heat a 7- or 8-inch omelet pan or skillet over medium heat for 1 minute. Add the butter and heat for 10 seconds or until the butter foams and begins to subside. Pour the egg mixture into the center of the pan, tilting the pan for even coverage. Cook for 10 seconds or until the bottom is just set. Cook, lifting the edge of the omelet gently with a flat rubber spatula as the eggs set to allow the uncooked eggs to flow underneath; do not stir. Cook for 1 to 2 minutes or until the eggs are almost set. Sprinkle with the bacon. Arrange the cheese slices down the center of the eggs. Layer the spinach over the cheese using tongs. Remove the pan from the heat. Using a spatula, turn one-third of the omelet nearest the handle over the filling in the center. Tilt the pan and guide the omelet with the spatula as it rolls onto a serving plate, forming a seam side down envelope. Serve immediately.

Serves 1

You were born God's original. Try not to be someone's copy.

—MARIAN WRIGHT EDELMAN

Boiled Egg in a Sausage Blanket

10 hard-cooked eggs
All-purpose flour
2 pounds bulk pork sausage
Salt and freshly cracked pepper to taste
2 eggs
2 tablespoons water
6 ounces dry bread crumbs
Vegetable oil for deep-frying

Cover the hard-cooked eggs with a small amount of flour. Season the sausage with salt and pepper and mix well. Divide the sausage into ten equal portions and place on a floured surface. Wrap each portion around the hard-cooked eggs to cover completely. Beat the eggs with the water in a bowl. Brush over the sausage-covered eggs and coat liberally with the bread crumbs. Deep-fry in the hot oil in a deep fryer for 6 minutes, turning frequently to cook evenly. Drain and cool slightly before serving. Store any leftovers in the refrigerator.

Serves 10

Children need models rather than critics.

—JOSEPH JOUBERT

Breakfast Sausage Casserole

1 1/2 pounds bulk pork sausage, crumbled
6 slices white bread
3 tablespoons butter, softened
2 cups (8 ounces) shredded sharp Cheddar cheese
5 eggs
2 cups half-and-half
1 teaspoon dry mustard
1 teaspoon salt

Brown the sausage in a skillet, stirring until crumbly; drain. Trim the bread and spread with the butter. Cut the bread into cubes. Layer the bread cubes, sausage and cheese in a greased 9×13-inch baking dish. Beat the eggs in a bowl. Add the half-and-half, dry mustard and salt and mix well. Pour over the layers. Chill for 8 hours or longer. Bake at 350 degrees for 40 to 45 minutes or until set and brown.

Serves 10

The strength of a nation is derived from the integrity of its homes.
—CONFUCIUS

Sausage and Hash Brown Muffins

1 pound bulk pork sausage
1 onion, chopped
2 cups frozen hash brown potatoes, thawed
1 cup (4 ounces) shredded Cheddar cheese
3 tablespoons all-purpose flour
8 eggs, beaten
1 cup ranch salad dressing
1/2 cup milk

Brown the sausage with the onion in a large skillet, stirring until the sausage is crumbly; drain and cool. Combine the sausage, potatoes and cheese in a large bowl and mix well. Stir in the flour. Add the eggs, salad dressing and milk and mix well. Fill greased muffin cups one-half full. Bake at 325 degrees for 15 to 20 minutes or until golden brown. (*Note: The sausage mixture, potatoes and cheese may be mixed 8 to 10 hours ahead and stored in the refrigerator until ready to finish the recipe. You may also bake in miniature muffin cups and reduce the baking time.*)

Serves 24 to 30

Be content with your lot; one cannot be first in everything.

—AESOP

Parade of Peppers Quiche

1 (1-crust) pie pastry
1 tablespoon olive oil
1/2 red bell pepper, sliced
1/2 yellow bell pepper, sliced
1/2 red onion, sliced
2 garlic cloves, minced
1/3 cup cilantro, minced
1/2 teaspoon cayenne pepper

1/2 teaspoon ground cumin
Salt and black pepper to taste
1 (3-ounce) can sliced black
   olives, drained
6 ounces Pepper Jack cheese,
   shredded
3 eggs
1 1/2 cups half-and-half

Line a quiche dish with the pastry. Heat the olive oil in a sauté pan. Add the bell peppers and sauté for 5 minutes. Add the onion and garlic and sauté for 5 minutes. Add the cilantro, cayenne pepper, cumin, salt and black pepper and mix well. Spread in the pastry-lined quiche dish. Layer the olives and cheese over the sautéed vegetables. Beat the eggs and half-and-half in a bowl. Pour over the layers. Bake at 375 degrees for 35 to 45 minutes or until set.

Serves 6 to 8

Everyone is in awe of the lion tamer in a cage with half a dozen lions—everyone but a school bus driver.

—ANONYMOUS

Soufflé of Grits and Greens

8 ounces turnip greens, tough
   stems removed
1/4 cup (1/2 stick) unsalted butter
1/2 sweet onion, chopped
1 garlic clove, chopped
1/4 cup chicken broth
1 3/4 cups milk
1/2 cup heavy cream
3/4 cup grits

White and pale parts from 3 green
   onions, chopped
1 1/2 teaspoons fresh thyme leaves
Salt and pepper to taste
1/2 cup (2 ounces) shredded
   Cheddar cheese
3 egg yolks
3 egg whites
1/2 cup (2 ounces) grated
   Parmesan cheese

Stack five or six leaves of the turnip greens and roll up tightly. Cut into thin diagonal strips. Repeat with the remaining turnip greens. Melt the butter in a large skillet over medium-high heat. Add the turnip greens, onion and garlic. Cook for 10 minutes or until the turnip greens are wilted, stirring occasionally. Add the broth. Reduce the heat to medium. Cook, partially covered, for 20 minutes or until the turnip greens are tender. Remove from the heat to cool. Pour the turnip green mixture into a sieve and drain well, pressing out any excess liquid. Place in a bowl and set aside.

Bring the milk and cream to a simmer in a heavy saucepan over medium heat. Stir in the grits, green onions and thyme gradually. Add salt and pepper. Reduce the heat to low. Cook, covered, for 20 minutes or until the liquid is absorbed, stirring frequently and adjusting the heat as needed to keep the grits cooking gently. Remove from the heat. Stir in the Cheddar cheese. Add to the turnip green mixture and mix well.

Beat the egg yolks in a small bowl lightly with a fork. Stir into the grits mixture. Beat the egg whites at high speed in a mixing bowl until stiff peaks form. Stir one-fourth of the egg whites into the grits mixture. Fold the grits mixture into the remaining egg whites. Pour into a lightly buttered 9×13-inch baking dish. Sprinkle with the Parmesan cheese. Bake on the center oven rack at 350 degrees for 40 minutes or until puffed and golden brown. Serve immediately.

Serves 6

We are the hero of our own story.
—MARY McCARTHY

Appetizers

Cooking Up Fun With Kids

SHINY PAINT

1 part liquid glue
1 part tempera paint

Mix the glue and paint in a bowl. Apply the mixture
to the intended surface with a brush or experiment
with other methods.

Let stand until dry. The paint will have a shiny
wet look when dry.

Q

Creole Poulet Patties with Tomato and Sweet Red Pepper Sauce

Patties

1 cup chopped sweet red peppers

1/2 cup chopped celery

4 to 6 green onions, chopped

3 tablespoons unsalted butter

2 pounds ground uncooked boneless
   skinless chicken breasts

2 cups fine dry bread crumbs

2 eggs, lightly beaten

1/2 cup heavy cream, light cream or
   half-and-half

2 tablespoons Creole mustard

1/4 cup fresh parsley, finely chopped

2 teaspoons finely crumbled
   dried tarragon

Salt and pepper to taste

2 tablespoons or more olive oil

**Tomato and Sweet Red
Pepper Sauce**

2 shallots or 1 small onion,
   finely chopped

1 sweet red pepper, chopped

1/4 cup (1/2 stick) unsalted butter

6 tomatoes, peeled, seeded
   and chopped

1/4 cup dry white wine

1/4 cup fresh parsley or thyme,
   finely chopped

Salt and cayenne pepper to taste

To prepare the patties, sauté the sweet peppers, celery and green onions in the butter in a sauté pan over medium heat for 6 minutes or until tender. Combine with the chicken, bread crumbs, eggs, cream, Creole mustard, parsley, tarragon, salt and pepper in a bowl and mix well. Chill for 2 to 24 hours. Shape 1 tablespoon of the chicken mixture at a time into a round patty 1/2 inch thick. Heat the olive oil in a sauté pan over medium-high heat. Carefully add the chicken patties a few at a time and fry for 4 minutes or until golden brown, turning once and adding additional olive oil as needed. Arrange on a baking sheet. Bake at 400 degrees for 6 minutes or until cooked through. Drain well on paper towels.

To prepare the sauce, sauté the shallots and sweet pepper in the butter in a sauté pan over medium heat for 5 minutes or until tender. Add the tomatoes. Cook for 8 minutes. Stir in the wine, parsley, salt and cayenne pepper. Keep warm until ready to serve. To serve, spoon a dollop of the sauce on top of each patty and garnish with a sprig of fresh parsley or a tarragon leaf.

Serves 8 to 12

You are unique, and if that is not fulfilled, then something has been lost.

—MARTHA GRAHAM

Crabby Patties

1/4 cup mayonnaise
1 egg
1 teaspoon baking powder
1 teaspoon Creole seasoning
1 teaspoon Worcestershire sauce
1 teaspoon Creole mustard
1/4 teaspoon salt
1/4 teaspoon parsley flakes
Dash of Creole sauce
1 cup bread crumbs or cracker crumbs
1 pound fresh jumbo lump crab meat,
    drained and shells removed
1/2 cup olive oil

Whisk the mayonnaise, egg, baking powder, Creole seasoning, Worcestershire sauce, Creole mustard, salt, parsley flakes and Creole sauce in a large bowl. Gently fold in the bread crumbs and crab meat, being careful not to break up the crab meat. Shape the mixture into six patties and place on a baking sheet. Chill, covered, for 1 hour or longer.

Heat the olive oil in a medium skillet over medium-high heat. Add the patties. Cook on each side for 3 to 4 minutes or until golden brown.

Serves 6

Your children will become what you are; so be what you want them to be.
—DAVID BLY

Crab Buttons with Creole Dipping Sauce

Crab Buttons
24 mushrooms
2 cups crab meat
1/4 cup fresh parsley, finely chopped
2 tablespoons bread crumbs
2 tablespoons finely chopped onion
2 tablespoons freshly grated Parmesan cheese
Creole seasoning to taste
2 eggs, lightly beaten
Louisiana hot pepper sauce to taste

Creole Dipping Sauce
1/4 cup mayonnaise
1 tablespoon Creole mustard
1 tablespoon fresh parsley, chopped (optional)

To prepare the crab buttons, remove the stems from the mushrooms, reserving the caps. Finely chop the mushroom stems. Combine the crab meat, mushroom stems, parsley, bread crumbs, onion, Parmesan cheese and Creole seasoning in a bowl and mix well. Add the eggs and hot pepper sauce and mix well. Stuff the crab meat mixture into the reserved mushroom caps. Place in a baking pan. Bake at 325 degrees for 20 to 30 minutes or until tender.

To prepare the sauce, combine the mayonnaise, Creole mustard and 1 tablespoon parsley in a small bowl and mix well. Serve with the hot mushroom caps.

Makes 24

My fathers planted for me, and I planted for my children.
—HEBREW PROVERB

Crawfish Cakes with Lemon Creole Aïoli

Lemon Creole Aïoli

1 cup mayonnaise

Juice of 1 large lemon

2 tablespoons fresh parsley,
 finely chopped

3/4 tablespoon Creole seasoning

Lemon zest to taste

Louisiana hot pepper sauce to taste

Salt and freshly cracked pepper
 to taste

Crawfish Cakes

1/2 cup finely chopped yellow onion

1/2 cup finely chopped green
 bell pepper

1/2 cup finely chopped celery

1 tablespoon finely chopped fresh garlic

2 tablespoons olive oil

1/4 cup cooking wine

1 pound Louisiana crawfish tails

3 eggs, beaten

2 sleeves saltine crackers

Louisiana blackened seasoning to taste

Salt and freshly cracked pepper
 to taste

Olive oil for sautéing

To prepare the sauce, combine the mayonnaise, lemon juice, parsley, Creole seasoning, lemon zest, hot pepper sauce, salt and pepper in a bowl and mix well.

To prepare the cakes, sauté the onion, bell pepper, celery and garlic in 2 tablespoons olive oil in a sauté pan over medium heat until the onion is translucent. Add the wine and crawfish tails. Cook for 10 minutes or until the alcohol cooks off. Remove from the heat and place in a mixing bowl. Let stand until room temperature. Add the eggs and mix well. Crush 1 1/2 sleeves of the crackers and add to the mixture. Add the blackened seasoning, salt and pepper and mix until of the consistency of a moist hamburger patty. Crush the remaining crackers and stir into the mixture. Shape into patties. Sauté in hot olive oil in a skillet until golden brown on both sides, firm to the touch and cooked through. Serve with the sauce.

Serves 6

Every artist was first an amateur.

—RALPH WALDO EMERSON

Mud Bug Corn Fritters

2 cups self-rising yellow cornmeal
1 cup self-rising flour
3 tablespoons sugar
$^1/_2$ teaspoon salt
3 eggs, beaten
$^1/_2$ cup milk
1 (16-ounce) can cream-style corn
1 large onion, finely chopped
2 jalapeño chiles, finely chopped
$^1/_2$ cup (2 ounces) shredded Cheddar cheese
$^1/_2$ cup (2 ounces) shredded Colby cheese
$^1/_2$ cup (2 ounces) shredded Monterey Jack cheese
1 pound cooked crawfish tails
Vegetable oil for frying

Mix the cornmeal, flour, sugar and salt in a large bowl. Add the eggs and milk and mix well. Stir in the corn, onion, chiles, Cheddar cheese, Colby cheese and Monterey Jack cheese. Wet your hands and roll the mixture into $1^1/_2$-inch balls. Stuff one crawfish tail into each ball. Fry in hot oil in a large skillet until golden brown. Remove from the oil and drain on paper towels.

Makes $3^1/_2$ dozen

Allow children to be happy in their own way, for what better way will they find?
—SAMUEL JOHNSON

LSU Sugar Bowl Shrimp Boats

1/4 cup (1/2 stick) unsalted butter
2 tablespoons olive oil
1 cup chopped onion
1 bunch green onions, chopped
2 ribs celery, chopped
1 cup sliced fresh mushrooms
1 1/2 pounds uncooked large
   shrimp, peeled

All-purpose flour for sprinkling
Creole seasoning to taste
2 egg yolks
2 cups heavy cream
12 oblong brown-and-serve rolls
Unsalted butter to taste
Shredded cheese to taste

Melt 1/4 cup butter with the olive oil in a skillet. Add the onion, green onions, celery and mushrooms. Sauté until the onion is translucent. Add the shrimp and additional butter if needed. Sauté until the shrimp turn pink. Sprinkle with the flour and Creole seasoning. Stir the egg yolks into the cream in a bowl. Pour over the shrimp mixture. Cook until the sauce is of a gravy consistency, stirring constantly.

Bake the rolls according to the package directions. Remove from the oven and carve a rectangular shape into the center of each roll to form a boat. Place butter to taste and cheese in the bottom of each "boat" and bake for 4 minutes. Spoon the shrimp mixture into the boats and sprinkle with additional cheese. Bake at 350 degrees until the cheese melts. (Note: The bread can be prepared ahead for tailgating and finished at the pre-game party.)

Serves 12

The best inheritance a parent can give to his children is a few minutes of their time each day.

—M. GRUNDLER

Fried Eggplant Smothered in Shrimp Rémoulade

Shrimp Rémoulade

1 cup extra-virgin olive oil
1/2 cup tarragon vinegar or vinegar
1/4 cup horseradish mustard
2 tablespoons ketchup
2 tablespoons paprika
1 garlic clove
1/2 cup chopped green onions
1/2 cup chopped celery
Louisiana hot pepper sauce to taste
Salt and pepper to taste
24 medium shrimp, poached, peeled
   and chilled

Fried Eggplant

1 small eggplant, peeled and cut into
   thin slices
Salt to taste
1 egg, beaten
All-purpose flour or cornmeal
   for dredging
Creole seasoning to taste
Extra-virgin olive oil for frying
Mixed salad greens

To prepare the shrimp rémoulade, process the olive oil, vinegar, mustard, ketchup, paprika, garlic, green onions, celery, hot pepper sauce, salt and pepper in a blender until thoroughly blended. Pour over the shrimp in a large bowl. Marinate, covered, in the refrigerator for 4 hours.

To prepare the eggplant, cook the eggplant in salted water in a saucepan for 10 minutes; drain. Dip the eggplant into the egg. Dredge in a mixture of flour and Creole seasoning. Fry in olive oil in a skillet until brown. Drain on paper towels.

To serve, place the eggplant on a serving plate lined with mixed salad greens. Top the eggplant with the shrimp rémoulade. Garnish with fresh parsley and a squeeze of fresh lemon.

Serves 4

Strength is a matter of the made-up mind.

—JOHN BEECHER

Fried Shrimp

1 (5-ounce) can evaporated milk
2 eggs
2 tablespoons vinegar
1 tablespoon baking powder
1 pound fresh shrimp, peeled and deveined
1 cup all-purpose flour
Creole seasoning to taste
Vegetable oil for frying

Combine the evaporated milk, eggs, vinegar and baking powder in a large bowl and mix well. Add the shrimp and stir to coat. Marinate, covered, in the refrigerator for 1 hour.

Drain the shrimp, discarding the marinade. Dip the shrimp in a mixture of the flour and Creole seasoning. Fry in hot oil in a large skillet until the shrimp are brown and float to the top. Drain on paper towels.

Serves 2

Whatever course you decide upon, there is always someone to tell you that you are wrong. There are always difficulties arising which tempt you to believe that your critics are right. To map out a course of action and follow it to an end requires courage.

—RALPH WALDO EMERSON

Savory and Sweet Coconut Shrimp

1 1/3 cups French-fried onions
1/3 cup flaked coconut
1 teaspoon curry powder (optional)
1 pound uncooked large shrimp, peeled and deveined
Salt and white pepper to taste
2 egg whites, beaten

Place the French-fried onions, coconut and curry powder in a sealable plastic bag. Seal the bag and lightly crush with your hands or a rolling pin. Shake to mix. Season the shrimp with salt and white pepper. Dip into the egg whites and coat with the onion mixture, pressing firmly to adhere. Place on a baking sheet. Bake at 400 degrees for 10 minutes or until the shrimp are cooked through and crispy. Serve with Pineapple-Mango Salsa (page 104) or purchase prepared salsa at your local grocery store.

Serves 4

Human beings are the only creatures that allow their children to come back home.

—BILL COSBY

Cher Bebe Shrimp Quiches

3 ounces mascarpone cheese or cream cheese, softened
$1/2$ cup (1 stick) unsalted butter, softened
$1^{1}/_{2}$ cups all-purpose flour
30 small shrimp, steamed and peeled
1 egg, beaten
$1/2$ cup heavy cream
$1^{1}/_{2}$ tablespoons brandy
$1/2$ teaspoon salt
$1/2$ teaspoon freshly cracked pepper
$1^{1}/_{2}$ teaspoons fresh dill weed, or
    $1/2$ teaspoon dried dill weed
$1^{2}/_{3}$ ounces Swiss cheese

Beat the mascarpone cheese and butter in a mixing bowl until smooth. Add the flour and mix well. Shape the dough into thirty 1-inch balls. Place in lightly greased $1^{3}/_{4}$-inch muffin cups and shape into shells. Prick the bottom and the side of each pastry shell with a fork. Bake at 400 degrees for 5 minutes. Remove from the oven and cool on a wire rack.

Reduce the oven temperature to 350 degrees. Place one shrimp in each shell. Combine the egg, cream, brandy, salt, pepper and dill weed in a bowl and mix well. Spoon about 2 teaspoons of the egg mixture over the shrimp in each shell. Slice the Swiss cheese into thirty small triangles. Place over the top of each shell. Bake for 20 minutes or until set. Cool and remove from the pan. (*Note: To prepare ahead, wrap the baked quiches in foil and freeze. To serve, place the frozen quiches on a baking sheet and bake at 375 degrees for 7 to 10 minutes to reheat.*)

Makes 30

Motherhood qualified me to let the child within come out and play.

—Christy Borgeld

Oysters Rockefeller with Turnip Greens

1/2 (10-ounce) package frozen
   turnip greens
6 small green onions
2 ribs celery
1/3 bunch parsley
1/3 head lettuce
1/2 cup (1 stick) butter, softened
1/4 cup bread crumbs
1 teaspoon anchovy paste
1 tablespoon Worcestershire sauce

1/8 teaspoon Louisiana hot
   pepper sauce
1 1/2 tablespoons absinthe or white
   wine (optional)
1/4 teaspoon salt
Rock salt
3 dozen oysters on the half shell
1/2 cup bread crumbs
1/4 cup (1 ounce) grated
   Parmesan cheese

Purée the turnip greens, green onions, celery, parsley and lettuce in a blender. Pour into a saucepan. Add the butter and 1/4 cup bread crumbs and mix well. Add the anchovy paste, Worcestershire sauce, hot pepper sauce, absinthe and 1/4 teaspoon salt. Cook over medium-low heat until heated through, stirring frequently.

Spread a thick bed of rock salt in a large baking pan. Bake at 450 degrees for 20 minutes. Remove from the oven. Maintain the oven temperature. Set the oysters on the half shell in the hot rock salt. Spread 2 tablespoons of the sauce over each oyster. Mix 1/2 cup bread crumbs and the Parmesan cheese in a bowl. Top each oyster with 1 teaspoon of the bread crumb mixture. Bake for 30 minutes. Broil 3 inches from the heat source until brown.

Serves 6

The test of the morality of a society is what it does for its children.
—DIETRICH BONHOEFFER

The Cowboys' Barbecue Boulets

2 pounds lean ground beef or veal
1 cup bread crumbs
1 teaspoon garlic powder
2 envelopes onion soup mix
2 teaspoons Worcestershire sauce
2 eggs
1 tablespoon (or more) olive oil
1 cup finely chopped onion
2 (6-ounce) cans tomato paste
2 garlic cloves, finely chopped
1/4 cup Worcestershire sauce
3 tablespoons red wine vinegar
1/2 cup packed brown sugar
1/2 cup sweet pickle relish
1/2 cup beef broth
2 teaspoons salt
2 teaspoons dry mustard

Combine the ground beef, bread crumbs, garlic powder, soup mix, 2 teaspoons Worcestershire sauce and the eggs in a bowl and mix well. Shape into meatballs. Brown in 1 tablespoon olive oil in a skillet, adding additional olive oil as needed. Drain on paper towels.

Combine the onion, tomato paste, garlic, 1/4 cup Worcestershire sauce, the vinegar, brown sugar, relish, broth, salt and dry mustard in a slow cooker and mix well. Add the meatballs. Cook, covered, on Low for 5 to 6 hours or on High for 2 to 3 hours.

Serves 60

Character is doing what's right when nobody is looking.

—J. C. WATTS, JR.

The Poke's Pistolettes

1 pound lean ground beef
1 onion, finely chopped
1 small sweet red pepper, finely chopped
1 large carrot, shredded
3/4 cup fresh whole kernel corn (1 large cob)
1 (14-ounce) can fire-roasted diced tomatoes
1/2 cup tomato paste
1/4 cup chicken broth
2 tablespoons rolled oats
1 tablespoon Worcestershire sauce
1 1/2 teaspoons chili powder
1 1/2 teaspoons ground cumin
1/2 teaspoon garlic powder
Shredded Cheddar cheese to taste
1 package pistolettes (French rolls)
Melted butter for brushing

Brown the ground beef with the onion, red pepper, carrot and corn in a large skillet, stirring until the ground beef is crumbly; drain. Stir in the undrained tomatoes, tomato paste, broth, oats, Worcestershire sauce, chili powder, cumin and garlic powder. Bring to a boil and reduce the heat. Simmer, uncovered, for 5 to 10 minutes or until of the desired consistency. Stir in the cheese.

Cut off the end of the pistolettes and hollow out the inside. Fill each with the ground beef mixture. Brush with butter on all sides. Place on a baking sheet. Bake at 350 degrees for 15 to 20 minutes or until golden brown.

Serves 4 to 6

A child's spirit is like a child, you can never catch it by running after it;
you must stand still, and, for love, it will soon itself come back.

—ARTHUR MILLER

"Mar-dee-graw" Mini-Meat Pies

12 ounces ground beef
4 ounces sweet Italian sausage
1 large sweet onion, chopped
1 1/2 cups sliced fresh mushrooms
1 (8-ounce) can tomato sauce
1 1/2 tablespoons Cajun seasoning
1/2 cup (2 ounces) shredded Monterey Jack cheese
3 (8-count) cans refrigerator biscuits
1 egg, lightly beaten
Vegetable oil for frying
Salsa to taste
Sour cream to taste

Brown the ground beef and Italian sausage in a large skillet over medium heat, stirring until crumbly. Drain, reserving 2 tablespoons of the drippings in the skillet. Sauté the onion in the reserved drippings for 5 minutes or until tender. Add the mushrooms and sauté for 2 minutes. Return the ground beef mixture to the skillet. Stir in the tomato sauce and Cajun seasoning. Simmer for 8 minutes or until the liquid evaporates, stirring occasionally. Remove from the heat to cool completely. Stir in the cheese. Chill, covered, in the refrigerator.

Roll each biscuit into a 4-inch circle on a lightly floured surface. Spoon 1 tablespoon of the ground beef mixture in the center of each circle. Brush the edge with the beaten egg and fold over, pressing with a fork to seal. Place on baking sheets and cover with a damp cloth. Chill for 2 hours or longer.

Fry the meat pies in batches in 1/2 inch hot oil in a Dutch oven for 30 seconds on each side or until golden brown. Drain on paper towels. Top with salsa and sour cream.

Serves 12

It is nice to be important, but it is more important to be nice.

—ANONYMOUS

Cochon de Lait Skewers

1¹/4 pounds pork tenderloin, cut into 20 (1-inch) cubes
20 (³/4-inch) cubes coarse country bread
16 (³/4-inch) squares bacon
3 tablespoons olive oil
³/4 teaspoon salt
¹/4 teaspoon pepper
¹/4 teaspoon chili powder
1 teaspoon chopped fresh sage

Combine the pork cubes, bread cubes, bacon and olive oil in a bowl and toss to mix. Add the salt, pepper, chili powder and sage and toss to coat evenly. Let stand for 5 minutes. Thread five cubes pork, five cubes bread and four squares bacon alternately onto each skewer, ending with the pork and bread. Place on a grill rack. Grill for 3 to 4 minutes on each side until the pork is light golden brown and cooked through, watching carefully to prevent the bread from burning. The bread should be golden and crisp. (Note: It is crucial to the success of the recipe that the bread be smaller than the pork to keep it from contacting the grill and burning.)

Serves 4

Life, love, and laughter—what priceless gifts to give our children.
—PHYLLIS DRYDEN

"Tiger Bait"

4 pounds andouille or smoked sausage
2 cups dry white wine
1/4 cup honey
2 teaspoons brown sugar
2 tablespoons mustard

Cut the andouille into slices 1/4 to 1/2 inch thick and place in a skillet. Combine the wine, honey, brown sugar and mustard in a bowl and mix well. Pour over the andouille. Cook, covered, over low heat until the andouille is tender.

Serves 12

Your tomorrow is often the result of today.

—ANONYMOUS

Jalapeño French Kisses

1 (16-ounce) package seasoned herb stuffing mix
20 canned whole jalapeño chiles
2 cups (8 ounces) shredded sharp Cheddar cheese
3 cups (12 ounces) shredded Monterey Jack cheese
1 pound bulk pork sausage
2 cups baking mix
2 eggs, lightly beaten

Process the stuffing mix in a food processor until ground; set aside.

Cut a slit lengthwise on one side of each chile, leaving the other side intact. Remove the seeds. Stuff each chile with about 2 teaspoons Cheddar cheese and pinch the edges to close; set aside. Combine the remaining Cheddar cheese, Monterey Jack cheese, sausage and baking mix in a bowl and mix well. Pinch off about 2 rounded tablespoonfuls of the dough at a time and shape into a patty. Place the stuffed chile in the center and wrap the dough around the chile. Dip in the eggs and dredge in the ground stuffing mix. Place on a lightly greased baking sheet. Chill, covered, for up to 2 hours or prepare in advance and freeze for up to 1 month. Bake at 375 degrees for 30 minutes or until golden brown.

Serves 10

Every child is an artist. The problem is how to remain an artist once we grow up.

—PABLO PICASSO

Cajun Chicken Bites with Peach Mustard

5 boneless skinless chicken breasts,
    cut into bite-size pieces
Creole seasoning to taste
2 tablespoons unsalted butter
2 tablespoons olive oil
$1^1/_2$ cups peach preserves
6 tablespoons Creole mustard or Dijon mustard

Sprinkle the chicken with Creole seasoning and let stand for 30 minutes. Heat the butter and olive oil in a sauté pan over medium-high heat. Add the chicken and sauté for 5 minutes or until cooked through. Remove with a slotted spoon to paper towels to drain.

Combine the peach preserves and Creole mustard in a small saucepan. Heat over low heat until the preserves melt and the mixture is thoroughly blended, stirring constantly. Remove from the heat to cool. Serve with the chicken as a dipping sauce.

Serves 8 to 10

A child becomes an adult when he realizes that he has a right not only to be right but also to be wrong.

—THOMAS SZASZ

Oven-Barbecued Lemon and Orange Chicken Drumettes

3/4 cup fresh orange juice
1/4 cup fresh lemon juice
1 cup packed brown sugar
1 (18-ounce) bottle barbecue sauce
40 chicken drumettes, trimmed (3 pounds)
3 small oranges, cut into quarters
2 or 3 lemons, cut into quarters

Combine the orange juice, lemon juice, brown sugar and barbecue sauce in a saucepan and mix well. Cook over medium heat for 10 minutes or until the brown sugar is dissolved and the flavors are blended.

Arrange the chicken in a single layer in a shallow ovenproof baking pan. Cut the orange and lemon quarters into thin slices. Alternate the orange and lemon slices between the chicken. Pour the sauce over the top. Bake, covered with a lid or foil, at 325 degrees for 1 hour. Bake, uncovered, for 30 minutes or until the chicken is tender and cooked through and the sauce is thickened. (*Note: Drumettes are the large portion of the chicken wings that look like a miniature drumstick. They may be found at your favorite grocery store or you may purchase whole chicken wings and disjoint, reserving the remaining wings to make chicken stock.*)

Serves 6 to 8

Children in a family are like flowers in a bouquet: there's always one determined to face in an opposite direction from the way the arranger desires.

—MARCELENE COX

Swashbucklers' Smoked Salmon
Deviled Egg Boats

12 hard-cooked eggs
1/2 cup finely chopped smoked salmon
1/2 cup cream cheese, softened
1/2 teaspoon garlic powder
1 tablespoon capers, chopped
Salt and white pepper to taste
Paprika to taste
3 (1-ounce) slices Swiss cheese

Peel the eggs and cut into halves lengthwise. Mash the egg yolks in a bowl. Add the salmon, cream cheese, garlic powder, capers, salt and white pepper and mix well. Spoon into the egg whites and place on a serving platter. Sprinkle with paprika. Cut each Swiss cheese slice into eight triangles. Push a wooden pick through the cheese triangle to resemble a "sail" and place one in each stuffed egg to resemble a boat. (Note: Make sure you pick Swiss cheese slices with lots of holes in them to represent tattered sails from cannon balls. For a variation, try this with your classic deviled egg recipe and for the sails cut red, yellow and green bell peppers into 1-inch wide strips. Then cut each strip into 1-inch squares. Cut each square into halves diagonally to make very colorful sails. These make a fantastic presentation for a pirate party or Fourth of July get-together.)

Makes 24

When I approach a child, he inspires in me two sentiments: tenderness for what he is, and respect for what he may become.

—LOUIS PASTEUR

Spinach Deviled Eggs

12 hard-cooked eggs
1/4 cup cream cheese, softened, or light mayonnaise
2 tablespoons vinegar
2 tablespoons butter, softened
1 tablespoon sugar
Salt and freshly cracked pepper to taste
1/2 cup frozen chopped spinach, thawed and squeezed dry
1 tablespoon finely chopped marinated artichoke hearts
4 slices bacon, cooked and crumbled
Grated Parmesan cheese to taste

Peel the eggs and cut into halves lengthwise. Mash the egg yolks in a bowl. Add the cream cheese, vinegar, butter, sugar, salt and pepper and mix well. Add the spinach and artichoke hearts and mix well. Stir in the bacon. Spoon into the egg whites. Sprinkle with Parmesan cheese.

Makes 24

He turns not back who is bound to a star.

—LEONARDO DA VINCI

Da' Cheesy Artichoke Squares

2 teaspoons butter
2 (6-ounce) jars marinated artichoke hearts
1/2 onion, minced
1 garlic clove, minced
4 eggs
1/4 cup fine dry bread crumbs
1/4 teaspoon salt
1/8 teaspoon dried oregano
1/8 teaspoon pepper
1/8 teaspoon Tabasco sauce
8 ounces natural sharp Cheddar cheese, shredded
2 tablespoons parsley, minced

Grease a 6×10-inch baking dish with the butter. Drain the marinade from one jar of the artichoke hearts into a small skillet. Add the onion and garlic. Cook gently until the onion is translucent. Drain the marinade from the remaining jar of artichoke hearts and reserve for later use as a salad dressing. Finely chop the artichoke hearts from both jars.

Beat the eggs lightly in a medium bowl. Stir in the bread crumbs, salt, oregano, pepper and Tabasco sauce. Add the cheese, parsley, artichoke hearts and onion mixture and mix well. Spoon into the prepared baking dish. Bake at 325 degrees for 30 minutes or until the center feels firm to the touch. Remove from the oven and let stand for 15 minutes. Cut into 1-inch squares. Serve warm or at room temperature.

Makes 72

Your family and your love must be cultivated like a garden.
Time, effort, and imagination must be summoned constantly to keep
any relationship flourishing and growing.

—KIM ROHN

Herbed-Stuffed Snow Peas

1 pound snow peas
2 (5-ounce) packages boursin herbed garlic cheese
2 tablespoons cream

Break the ends off the snow peas and pull the strings from the straight side of the peas. Blanch the peas in boiling water in a saucepan for 1 minute; drain. Place the peas immediately in ice water in a bowl to stop the cooking process. Mix the cheese and cream in a bowl until smooth and creamy. Place in a pastry bag fitted with the desired tip.

Slit the straight side of each of the snow peas to open. Pipe the cheese mixture into the peas and arrange on a serving plate. Chill, covered, until serving time.

Serves 6 to 8

Do whatever you do intensely.
—ROBERT HENRI

Phyllo Triangles with a Three-Cheese Medley

Olive oil

1 cup whole-milk ricotta cheese

6 ounces feta cheese, crumbled

6 ounces smoked mozzarella cheese,
    cut into 1/4-inch cubes

3 small shallots, minced

1/3 cup fresh flat-leaf parsley,
    coarsely chopped

1 egg, lightly beaten

Salt and pepper to taste

7 sheets frozen phyllo, thawed

1/3 cup unsalted butter, melted

Grease one or two baking sheets lightly with olive oil. Combine the ricotta cheese, feta cheese, mozzarella cheese, shallots, parsley, egg, salt and pepper in a bowl and toss with your hands until blended. Cut the phyllo into quarters lengthwise to form strips about 3 1/2 inches wide. Keep the phyllo covered with waxed paper topped with a damp towel to keep it from drying out, removing one sheet at a time.

Place one phyllo strip on a dry work surface and brush lightly but thoroughly with the melted butter. Place 1 tablespoon of the cheese mixture about 1 inch from the bottom edge. Fold the lower right corner up and over the filling to form a triangle. Fold the triangle straight forward and then again on a diagonal. Continue folding and forming a triangle each time until you reach the end of the strip. Place on the prepared baking sheet and brush with the melted butter. Repeat the process with the remaining phyllo strips, butter and cheese mixture.

Bake at 350 degrees for 20 minutes or until golden brown. Cool for 10 minutes before serving. (Note: The triangles can be prepared up to 1 week ahead before baking. Place in an airtight container separated with waxed paper and store in the freezer. Bake the frozen triangles as above, adding an additional 5 to 7 minutes to the baking time.)

Makes 28

It takes a whole village to raise a child.

—AFRICAN PROVERB

Goat Cheese and Homegrown Tomato Tarts with Basil

20 fresh basil leaves, cut into
  thin strips
2 garlic cloves, finely chopped
2 cups grape tomatoes,
  cut into halves
1/4 cup extra-virgin olive oil
Salt to taste
1 (10×12-inch) sheet frozen puff
  pastry, partially thawed

5 ounces fresh goat cheese
1/2 cup (about) milk
1 large red tomato
1 large yellow tomato
6 tomatoes, cut into quarters
Freshly cracked pepper to taste
Extra-virgin olive oil for drizzling

Combine two-thirds of the basil strips, the garlic and grape tomatoes in a small bowl. Add 1/4 cup olive oil and salt and toss lightly to coat; set aside.

Place the puff pastry on a lightly floured cutting board. Cut into six 4×5-inch rectangles. Place the rectangles on a baking sheet and prick all over with a fork to prevent the pastry from rising. Bake on the center oven rack at 400 degrees for 10 minutes or until light golden brown. Remove from the oven and let stand on the baking sheet. Maintain the oven temperature.

Mash the goat cheese with a fork in a small bowl. Add enough of the milk to form a smooth but not runny consistency. Cut the large red and yellow tomatoes into slices 1/2 inch thick, discarding the ends. Sprinkle with salt and pepper. Gently spread 1 1/2 tablespoons of the goat cheese mixture onto each pastry rectangle and top with a tomato slice. Bake for 5 minutes or until heated through. Place the tarts on individual serving plates.

Sprinkle the tomato quarters with salt and pepper. Scatter evenly around each tart. Mound the grape tomato mixture on top of each tart, dividing evenly. Drizzle olive oil over the tomatoes and top with the remaining basil strips. Serve immediately.

Serves 6

A man's work is from sun to sun, but a mother's work is never done.

—ANONYMOUS

Garden Fresh Tea Sandwiches

2 tablespoons red wine vinegar
2 tablespoons extra-virgin olive oil
Salt and pepper to taste
1 large cucumber, peeled and thinly sliced
12 radishes, thinly sliced
1/2 cup (1 stick) unsalted butter, softened
2 tablespoons finely chopped chives
20 slices sandwich bread, crusts trimmed

Whisk the vinegar and olive oil in a bowl until emulsified. Season with salt and pepper. Add the cucumber and radishes and toss to coat. Combine the butter and chives in a small bowl and mix well. Season with salt and pepper.

Spread each bread slice with the butter mixture. Divide the cucumber mixture among one-half of the bread slices. Top with the remaining bread slices and press gently. Cut each sandwich diagonally into halves. Arrange on a serving platter and serve immediately.

Serves 20

You know children are growing up when they start asking questions that have answers.

—JOHN J. PLOMP

Melon Balls in a Prosciutto Blanket

1 small honeydew melon, cut into halves and seeded
1 small cantaloupe, cut into halves and seeded
1 small watermelon, cut into halves and seeded
8 slices prosciutto (about 4 ounces)
Freshly ground pepper to taste (optional)

Scoop sixteen balls from each melon using the large end of a melon baller, for a total of forty-eight balls. Reserve the remaining melons for another purpose. Cut each prosciutto slice lengthwise into thirds and then crosswise into halves to make six strips, for a total of forty-eight strips. Chill the melon balls and prosciutto until ready to assemble and serve.

To serve, wrap a strip of prosciutto around each melon ball. Secure with cocktail picks, if desired. Sprinkle with pepper. *(Note: Do not refrigerate after wrapping or the juice from the melons will discolor the prosciutto and make it soggy.)*

Makes 48

One thought driven home is better than three left on base.

—JAMES LITER

Trio of Cheese Fondue with Grilled Fruit

Mascarpone Cheese
8 ounces cream cheese, softened
2 teaspoons butter, softened
1/4 cup whipping cream

Fondue
1 large garlic clove, cut into
    halves lengthwise
1 (8-ounce) log goat cheese
1/4 cup milk
1/2 cup crumbled blue cheese

Salt and freshly cracked pepper
to taste

Grilled Fruit
2 mangoes, pitted, peeled and
    cut into 1/2-inch pieces
1/2 small pineapple, cored and cut
    into 1/2-inch pieces
2 nectarines, peeled and
    cut into quarters
2 tablespoons lemon-infused olive oil

To prepare the mascarpone cheese, beat the cream cheese and butter in a mixing bowl until smooth. Add the whipping cream and beat well.

To prepare the fondue, rub the inside of a ceramic fondue pot with the cut sides of the garlic and discard. Place the mascarpone cheese, goat cheese and milk in the prepared fondue pot. Heat over medium heat for 5 minutes or until the cheeses melt, stirring constantly. Add the blue cheese, salt and pepper. Continue to heat until the mixture is creamy and well blended, stirring constantly.

To prepare the fruit, place the mango and pineapple pieces and nectarine quarters in a bowl. Drizzle with the olive oil, turning gently to coat evenly. Arrange the fruit in a single layer in a grill basket. Grill over medium-high heat for 5 minutes or until the outside of the fruit begins to caramelize, turning once or twice.

To serve, arrange the fruit on a serving platter. Dip the fruit into the fondue using fondue forks. (*Note: Mascarpone cheese can also be purchased prepared in some grocery stores.*)

Serves 4

Silent gratitude isn't much use to anyone.

—G. B. STERN

Cheese Ball with Tabasco Pepper Jelly

2 cups pecans, chopped
1 cup chopped green onion tops
2 cups (8 ounces) finely grated Cheddar cheese
1 cup mayonnaise
1 (10-ounce) jar Tabasco pepper jelly

Combine the pecans, green onion tops, cheese and mayonnaise in a bowl and mix well. Shape into a ball on a serving plate. Chill, covered, for 1 hour or longer. Pour the pepper jelly on top of the cheese ball just before serving. Serve with crackers or corn chips.

Serves 6 to 8

*Too many people overvalue what they are not
and undervalue what they are.*

—MALCOM FORBES

Fantastic Figue Caponata

1 pound eggplant
2 tablespoons chopped shallots
3 garlic cloves, minced
1/2 cup finely chopped dried figs (about 5 whole figs)
1/2 cup water
2 tablespoons white wine vinegar
2 teaspoons fresh lemon juice
1 tablespoon brown sugar
1/2 teaspoon salt
1/4 teaspoon crushed red pepper
2 teaspoons fresh lemon juice
1/4 cup toasted pine nuts
1 tablespoon parsley, chopped

Cut the eggplant lengthwise into halves. Place cut sides down on a baking sheet coated with nonstick cooking spray. Bake at 450 degrees for 20 minutes or until the eggplant is tender and the cut sides are brown. Remove from the oven and let cool completely. Carefully remove and discard the skin from the eggplant with a fork. Finely chop the eggplant and place in a bowl.

Sauté the shallots and garlic in a large nonstick skillet coated with nonstick cooking spray over medium-high heat for 2 minutes or until tender. Stir in the figs, water, vinegar, 2 teaspoons lemon juice, the brown sugar, salt and red pepper. Simmer for 5 minutes or until the liquid almost evaporates. Remove from the heat. Add the eggplant and mix well. Stir in 2 teaspoons lemon juice, the pine nuts and parsley.

Serves 10

*The nice thing about teamwork is that you
always have others on your side.*

—MARGARET CARTY

Tuna Ceviche

2 tablespoons coconut milk
1 tablespoon fresh lime juice
1 serrano chile, finely sliced
1/2 teaspoon sugar
1/2 teaspoon grated ginger
1 small bunch watercress, chopped
10²/3 ounces sushi grade tuna, finely chopped
1/4 cup cilantro, chopped
2 tablespoons minced red onion
1 tablespoon extra-virgin olive oil
Sea salt to taste

Combine the coconut milk, lime juice, chile, sugar and ginger in a bowl and mix well. Chill, covered, until serving time. Fold in the watercress, tuna, cilantro, red onion, olive oil and sea salt just before serving. Serve with crackers.

Serves 12

I am seeking; I am striving; I am in it with all my heart.

—VINCENT VAN GOGH

Pepper Jack Baked Crab Dip

Roasted Garlic
1 head garlic
Olive oil for drizzling

Dip
3/4 cup mayonnaise
1/4 cup minced green onions
3 tablespoons Worcestershire sauce
2 tablespoons fresh lemon or
    lime juice

1 1/2 teaspoons Creole hot
    pepper sauce
1/2 teaspoon dry mustard
Salt and pepper to taste
1 pound jumbo lump crab meat
1 cup (4 ounces) shredded Pepper
    Jack cheese
1/4 cup (1 ounce) grated
    Parmesan cheese

To prepare the garlic, peel the outer layers of the garlic skin of 1 head garlic, leaving the skins of the individual cloves intact. Cut off 1/4 to 1/2 inch of the top of the cloves until the individual cloves of garlic are exposed. Place the head of garlic in a small ovenproof baking dish. Drizzle with olive oil, using your fingers to make sure the entire garlic head is well coated. Bake, covered with foil, at 400 degrees for 30 minutes or until the cloves feel soft when pressed. Let stand until cool enough to handle.

To prepare the dip, remove five or six cloves of the roasted garlic to a bowl, reserving the remaining garlic for another purpose. Mash the garlic. Add the mayonnaise, green onions, Worcestershire sauce, lemon juice, hot pepper sauce, dry mustard, salt and pepper and mix well. Gently stir in the crab meat, Pepper Jack cheese and Parmesan cheese. Spoon into a baking dish. Bake at 325 degrees for 40 minutes. Serve with crackers or toast.

Makes 4 cups

Before I got married, I had six theories about bringing up children;
now I have six children and no theories.

—JOHN WILMOT, EARL OF ROCHESTER

Soups

Cooking Up Fun With Kids

FLUBBER

1½ cups warm water
2 cups white glue
Food coloring
1⅓ cups warm water
1 tablespoon borax

Combine 1½ cups warm water, the glue and food coloring in a
large pail or other large container and mix well.

Combine 1⅓ cups warm water and the borax in a small container
and mix well.

Pour the borax mixture into the glue mixture. Gently lift and turn
the mixture until only about 1 tablespoon
of liquid remains.

The Flubber will be sticky for awhile. Let the excess liquid drip off.
Then the Flubber will be ready.

Shrimp and Crab Corn Chowder

1 red bell pepper
1 cup (or more) chicken broth
1 cup chopped celery
1 cup chopped leek or onion
1/2 cup brown rice
1/2 cup pearl barley
1 1/2 pounds small to medium shrimp, peeled
1 1/2 pounds crab meat
1 1/2 cups fresh whole kernel corn
    (from about 3 ears)
1/2 cup heavy cream
Salt and white pepper to taste
Nutmeg to taste

Char the bell pepper over an open flame on all sides. Place in a loosely closed paper bag. Let stand for 15 minutes or until cool. Remove from the bag and rub off the blackened skin with your fingertips. Cut the bell pepper into halves. Remove and discard the seeds and veins. Cut the bell pepper into thin pieces.

Combine the broth, celery and leek in a stockpot. Cook, covered, over medium heat for 25 minutes or until the vegetables are soft. Add the rice and barley. Simmer, covered, for 40 minutes or until the grains are soft. Purée in a blender or food processor until smooth. Strain through a medium fine mesh strainer into a saucepan, discarding the solids. Stir in the shrimp, crab meat, corn and cream. Add additional broth if needed for a thick creamy consistency. Season with salt and white pepper. Simmer over low heat for 15 to 20 minutes or until the shrimp turn pink. Do not boil. Ladle into soup bowls. Top each serving with the roasted bell pepper and nutmeg.

Serves 8

There are no seven wonders of the world in the eyes
of a child. There are seven million.

—WALT STREIGHTIFF

"The Fais-do-do" Frogmore Stew

6 quarts water
1 lemon, cut into halves
1 (4-ounce) package dry crawfish, shrimp and crab boil
2 garlic cloves, crushed
1 onion, cut into halves
2 pounds new potatoes
2 pounds smoked sausage, cut into 1/2-inch slices
10 to 12 ears of corn, broken into 3-inch pieces
4 pounds uncooked unpeeled shrimp
Salt to taste

Pour the water into a large stockpot. Squeeze the juice from the lemon halves into the water and then add the lemon halves. Stir in the crab boil, garlic and onion. Bring to a boil. Add the potatoes and cook for 15 minutes. Add the sausage. Boil gently for 10 minutes. Add the corn and cook for 5 minutes. Add the shrimp and cook for 3 to 5 minutes or until the shrimp turn pink. Remove from the heat and drain. Season with salt and serve.

Serves 8

Let your life be like a snowflake, leave a mark but not a stain.
—ANONYMOUS

Pumpkin Oyster Soup

1 (16-ounce) can pumpkin
6 cups chicken broth
Salt and pepper to taste
3/4 cup dry sherry
1/2 pint shelled oysters and liquid
1 cup heavy cream
Nutmeg to taste

Bring the pumpkin and broth to a simmer in a large saucepan. Season with salt and pepper. Stir in the sherry. Add the oysters and cream. Cook until the edges of the oysters curl and the soup is heated through. Ladle into soup bowls and sprinkle with nutmeg.

Serves 4 to 6

Truthfulness is the main element of character.

—BRIAN TRACY

Snappy Turtle Soup

2 quarts (or more) water
1¹/2 pounds turtle meat
1 bay leaf
Sea salt or salt to taste
¹/4 cup (¹/2 stick) unsalted butter
¹/4 cup chopped celery
¹/4 cup chopped onion
¹/4 cup chopped bell pepper
¹/2 cup fresh parsley, finely chopped
¹/4 teaspoon finely chopped garlic

¹/4 cup tomato paste
2 tablespoons Worcestershire sauce
Salt and freshly cracked pepper
   to taste
¹/2 cup all-purpose flour
Louisiana hot pepper sauce to taste
¹/2 cup sherry
2 medium hard-cooked eggs,
   finely chopped

Bring 2 quarts water, the turtle meat, bay leaf and sea salt to a boil in a 3¹/2-quart stockpot over high heat. Reduce the heat to medium and cook for 1 hour or until the turtle meat is tender, adding additional water as needed to maintain 1¹/2 quarts liquid throughout the cooking process. Remove the turtle meat to a plate and finely chop. Cover and set aside. Strain the remaining stock into a large bowl, discarding the solids; set aside.

Melt the butter in a 5¹/2-quart Dutch oven. Add the celery, onion, bell pepper, parsley, garlic, tomato paste, Worcestershire sauce, salt and pepper. Sauté until the vegetables are tender. Stir in the flour. Cook over medium heat until all of the liquid is absorbed by the flour, stirring constantly and watching carefully to prevent burning. Add the reserved stock and bring to a boil. Add the turtle meat. Reduce the heat to low and cook for 45 minutes. Remove and discard the bay leaf. Stir in the hot pepper sauce and sherry. Ladle into soup bowls and sprinkle each serving with the eggs. Garnish with thinly sliced lemon wedges. (Note: Ground veal shank can be substituted for the turtle meat if green just ain't yo thang!)

Serves 4 to 6

Why not go out on a limb? Isn't that where the fruit is?

—FRANK SKULLY

Southwest Louisiana Chicken Tortilla Soup

2 (14-ounce) cans chicken broth
1 (14-ounce) can Cajun-style stewed tomatoes
1 small onion, chopped
2 tablespoons fresh lemon juice
3 garlic cloves, pressed
2 teaspoons chili powder
1/2 teaspoon ground cumin
1/4 teaspoon red pepper
1 1/2 cups chopped cooked chicken
1 cup fresh or frozen whole kernel corn
1 (15-ounce) can black beans, drained and rinsed
2 tablespoons half-and-half
1 to 2 cups (4 to 8 ounces) shredded Mexican
    four-cheese blend (optional)
Chopped green onions to taste

Bring the broth, tomatoes, onion, lemon juice, garlic, chili powder, cumin and red pepper to a boil in a stockpot and reduce the heat. Add the chicken, corn, black beans and half-and-half. Simmer for 20 minutes. Ladle into soup bowls. Sprinkle each serving with the cheese and green onions. Serve with tortilla chips.

Serves 4

A joyful heart is the inevitable result of a heart burning with love.

—MOTHER TERESA

White Bean Chicken Chili

1 pound dried Great Northern beans
1 large onion, chopped
1 teaspoon minced garlic
1 tablespoon finely chopped
    jalapeño chile
1 tablespoon dried oregano
Dash of cayenne pepper
2 teaspoons ground cumin
1 green bell pepper, chopped
1 tablespoon chili powder
5 cups chicken broth or stock
1 (10-ounce) can diced tomatoes
    with green chiles

1/4 cup lime juice
3 cups chopped grilled or
    cooked chicken
1 cup fresh or frozen whole kernel
    corn (optional)
1/2 cup fresh cilantro, finely chopped
1/3 cup shredded sharp
    Cheddar cheese
Chopped jalapeño chiles to taste
1 tomato, chopped
Sour cream

Sort and rinse the beans. Soak the beans in water to cover in a bowl for 8 to 10 hours. Drain and rinse the beans. Place in a large stockpot and cover with water. Add the onion, garlic, 1 tablespoon jalapeño chile, the oregano, cayenne pepper, cumin, bell pepper, chili powder and broth. Bring to a boil and reduce the heat. Simmer, uncovered, for 1 1/2 hours. Add the tomatoes with green chiles, lime juice, chicken and corn. Cook, covered, over low heat for 30 minutes. Ladle into soup bowls. Sprinkle each serving with the cilantro, cheese, jalapeño chiles to taste and tomato. Top with a dollop of sour cream. Garnish with tortilla strips.

Serves 6 to 8

High achievement always takes place in the framework of high expectation.
—CHARLES KETTERING

Chicken and Sausage Gumbo

1 (3-pound) chicken, cut into
    serving pieces
Creole seasoning to taste
1 tablespoon plus 1/2 cup vegetable oil
1/2 cup all-purpose flour
1 cup coarsely chopped celery
1 cup coarsely chopped green
    bell pepper
1 cup coarsely chopped onion
3 garlic cloves, finely chopped
2 pounds smoked sausage of choice,
    cut into 1/2-inch-thick pieces

9 cups chicken broth
1 pound fresh okra, cut into 1/8-inch-
    thick pieces (optional)
1 cup chopped green onions
1/4 cup chopped parsley (optional)
1 1/2 teaspoons dried thyme,
    finely crumbled
6 to 8 cups cooked brown or
    white rice
Filé powder to taste
Louisiana hot pepper sauce to taste

Sprinkle the chicken with Creole seasoning. Sauté in 1 tablespoon oil in a 7 1/2-quart stockpot over medium-high heat for 5 to 6 minutes or until brown. Remove the chicken to a platter, reserving the pan drippings. Stir 1/2 cup oil and the flour into the reserved pan drippings to form a roux. Cook over medium heat for 20 to 25 minutes or until the roux is dark brown, stirring constantly. Add the celery, bell pepper, onion and garlic. Cook for 5 minutes or until the vegetables are wilted, stirring constantly. Add the sausage and Creole seasoning. Cook for 2 minutes, stirring frequently. Stir in the broth gradually. Bring to a boil and reduce the heat to medium-low. Add the okra, green onions, parsley and thyme. Cook for 1 hour, stirring occasionally. Return the chicken to the stockpot. Simmer for 1 1/2 hours, skimming off any fat that rises to the surface. Remove the chicken from the stockpot. Chop the chicken, discarding the skin and bones. Return the chicken to the gumbo. Ladle over the hot rice in serving bowls. Sprinkle with filé powder and hot pepper sauce.

Serves 8 to 10

*Andouille is gumbo sausage for all you peoples who live away
from the center of the universe.*

—JUSTIN WILSON

Chicken and Ham Stew

1/4 cup all-purpose flour
3 pounds chicken pieces
    (breasts, thighs and drumsticks),
    skin and fat removed
1/4 cup olive oil
1 tablespoon all-purpose flour
2 tablespoons finely chopped
    fresh garlic
5 cups chicken broth
1 (14-ounce) can stewed tomatoes,
    coarsely chopped
1 (6-ounce) can tomato paste
1 small onion, chopped

1 1/2 teaspoons Creole seasoning
1 1/2 teaspoons ground cumin
4 sprigs of oregano
4 sprigs of thyme
1 bay leaf
1/4 teaspoon crushed red pepper flakes
8 ounces chopped ham
2 cups cubed peeled new potatoes
2 cups chopped yellow squash
2 cups chopped carrots
2 cups chopped zucchini
8 ounces fresh or frozen whole
    kernel corn

Place 1/4 cup flour in a sealable plastic bag. Add the chicken and shake to coat. Heat the olive oil in a stockpot or Dutch oven. Add the chicken and cook until brown. Remove the chicken and set aside. Drain the stockpot, reserving 1 teaspoon of the drippings in the stockpot. Whisk 1 tablespoon flour and the garlic into the reserved drippings for 30 seconds. Stir in the broth, tomatoes, tomato paste, onion, Creole seasoning, cumin, oregano, thyme, bay leaf and red pepper flakes. Bring to a boil and reduce the heat. Simmer, uncovered, for 20 minutes. Return the chicken to the stockpot and add the ham. Simmer, covered, for 20 minutes. Skim off any fat that rises to the surface. Add the potatoes, squash, carrots, zucchini and corn. Simmer, covered, for 30 minutes. Remove and discard the bay leaf. Ladle into soup bowls. Garnish with cilantro.

Serves 6

Do not let what you cannot do interfere with what you can do.

—JOHN WOODEN

Burgundy Beef Stew with Feta Cheese

1/4 cup extra-virgin olive oil

1 1/2 pounds boneless beef chuck, cut into 1 1/2-inch cubes

2 tablespoons all-purpose flour

12 ounces small white onions

1 pound tomatoes, peeled, seeded and chopped

3 garlic cloves, minced

1 1/2 tablespoons fresh thyme, chopped

2 1/2 tablespoons fresh rosemary, chopped

2 1/2 tablespoons fresh oregano, chopped

1 bay leaf, crumbled

1 teaspoon ground cumin

2 to 3 cups dry red wine

8 ounces feta cheese, crumbled

Salt and freshly cracked pepper to taste

Heat the olive oil in a heavy 4- or 5-quart Dutch oven over medium-high heat. Toss the beef in the flour to coat. Cook the beef in batches in the hot olive oil for 3 minutes or until brown, stirring occasionally. Remove the beef to a bowl, reserving the pan drippings. Add the onions to the pan drippings. Cook for 5 minutes or until light brown, stirring frequently. Add the tomatoes, garlic, thyme, rosemary, oregano, bay leaf and cumin. Stir in the wine. Return the beef to the Dutch oven. Bring to a boil. Bake, covered, at 350 degrees for 2 hours or until the beef is tender. Stir in the cheese. Bake for 10 minutes or until the cheese is heated through. Add salt and pepper. Ladle into soup bowls.

Serves 4

Each child comes with the message that God is not yet discouraged of man.

—RABINDRANATH TAGORE

Andouille Wild Rice Soup

1 tablespoon butter
8 ounces andouille, cut into cubes
1 onion, chopped
1 carrot, coarsely shredded
2 ribs celery, chopped
1/2 green bell pepper, chopped
1 tablespoon all-purpose flour
1/4 teaspoon pepper
1 1/2 cups wild rice, cooked
1 cup water
2 cups chicken broth
1 cup half-and-half
1/3 cup slivered almonds
3 tablespoons fresh parsley, chopped
Salt to taste

Heat the butter in a stockpot. Add the andouille, onion, carrot, celery and bell pepper. Sauté over medium heat for 4 minutes. Add the flour and pepper. Stir in the cooked rice, water and broth. Bring to a boil and reduce the heat. Simmer for 15 minutes. Remove from the heat. Add the half-and-half gradually, stirring constantly. Add the almonds, parsley and salt. Return to the heat and cook until heated through; do not boil. Ladle into soup bowls. (*Note: For a vegetarian soup, omit the andouille and use vegetable broth instead of the chicken broth.*)

Serves 4

It is good to get what we want, but better to want what we get.

—ANONYMOUS

The Cowgirls' Cream of Broccoli Soup

1 quart chicken stock
1 cup dry white wine
4 cups broccoli cuts
1 tablespoon lemon juice
1 tablespoon Worcestershire sauce
1/2 teaspoon salt
1/2 teaspoon cayenne pepper
1/2 cup (1 stick) butter
1 cup evaporated milk
Shredded cheese to taste

Combine the stock, wine, broccoli, lemon juice, Worcestershire sauce, salt and cayenne pepper in a saucepan and mix well. Bring to a boil and reduce the heat. Simmer for 1 hour or until the broccoli is tender. Remove from the heat to cool. Purée in a blender.

To serve, heat the puréed broccoli mixture, butter and evaporated milk in a saucepan just to the boiling point or until the butter melts. Ladle into soup bowls and sprinkle each serving with shredded cheese.

Serves 8

Never mess up an apology with an excuse.
—ANONYMOUS

Bourbon Street Cheese and Ale Soup

1/2 cup (1 stick) unsalted butter
White and pale green part of 1 leek,
    rinsed and thinly sliced
1 carrot, peeled and cut into 1/2-inch-thick pieces
1 rib celery, rinsed and cut into 1/2-inch pieces
Salt and pepper to taste
1/2 cup all-purpose flour
1/2 teaspoon dry mustard
4 cups chicken stock
1 (12-ounce) bottle ale, such as Newcastle
2 cups (8 ounces) shredded sharp Cheddar cheese
1/4 cup (1 ounce) freshly grated Parmesan cheese
Pinch of cayenne pepper
1 teaspoon Worcestershire sauce
2 tablespoons finely chopped fresh flat-leaf parsley

Melt the butter in a large saucepan over medium heat. Add the leek, carrot and celery. Sauté for 8 to 10 minutes or until the vegetables are soft. Season with salt and pepper. Stir in the flour and dry mustard. Cook for 1 minute. Add the stock and ale. Bring to a simmer over high heat and reduce the heat to medium. Continue to cook, whisking constantly to break up any lumps of flour. Cook for 5 to 6 minutes or until slightly thickened, whisking constantly. Add the Cheddar cheese and Parmesan cheese. Cook for 3 to 4 minutes or until melted, whisking constantly. Do not boil or the soup may become stringy in texture. Stir in the cayenne pepper and Worcestershire sauce. Add the parsley and adjust the seasonings to taste. Ladle into soup bowls.

Serves 4 to 6

The achievement of your goal is assured the
moment you commit yourself to it.

—MACK R. DOUGLAS

"Onyon" Soup with Baguettes

Baguettes

1 envelope dry yeast

1 tablespoon sugar

2 teaspoons kosher salt or salt

2 cups warm water

4 cups (or more) cake flour

1 egg

Soup

4 Vidalia onions, sliced

1 tablespoon olive oil

1/4 cup (1/2 stick) unsalted butter

1 cup dry white wine

3 (14-ounce) cans beef broth

1 teaspoon Worcestershire sauce

3 garlic cloves, thinly sliced

1 teaspoon fresh thyme leaves,
    finely chopped

Salt and freshly cracked pepper to taste

Butter for spreading

4 slices Gruyère cheese

1 cup (4 ounces) shredded
    Gruyère cheese

To prepare the baguettes, dissolve the yeast, sugar and kosher salt in the warm water in a large bowl. Let stand for 10 minutes. Stir in the flour. Lift and turn the dough on a floured surface until the dough sticks together, adding additional flour if needed. Knead for 10 minutes or until smooth and elastic. Let rise, covered, in a bowl in a warm place for 45 minutes or until doubled in bulk. Pat the dough flat on a floured surface and dust with additional flour. Fold in half and then fold in half again. Return to the bowl. Let rise for 30 minutes. Place the dough on a floured surface and divide into four equal portions. Roll each portion into a ball. Let rest for 5 minutes. Shape each ball into an oval and roll up as for a jellyroll. Place on a greased baking sheet. Let rise until almost doubled in bulk. Brush each loaf with a mixture of the egg and a small amount of water. Bake at 450 degrees for 20 to 25 minutes or until golden brown. Cool and slice.

To prepare the soup, sauté the onions in the olive oil and 1/4 cup butter in a 5-quart Dutch oven over medium-low heat for 10 minutes or until the onions are golden brown. Add the wine, broth, Worcestershire sauce, garlic and thyme. Simmer over low heat for 45 minutes. Season with salt and pepper. To serve, spread four baguette slices with butter and place on a baking sheet. Bake at 425 degrees until toasted. Ladle the soup into four large ovenproof soup bowls and top each with a slice of the cheese. Top with a toasted baguette slice and the shredded cheese. Broil for 10 minutes or until the cheese melts.

Serves 4

To err is human, to forgive divine.

—ALEXANDER POPE

La Crème de la Crème Potato Soup

4 potatoes, chopped (about 2 cups)
2 small onions, sliced
2 ribs celery, finely chopped
2 cups chicken broth
2 cups milk
2 cups half-and-half
Salt and white pepper to taste
2 tablespoons butter
1 tablespoon fresh parsley, finely chopped
Paprika to taste

Place the potatoes, onions, celery and broth in a large saucepan. Cook, covered, over medium heat for 20 minutes or until the potatoes are soft. Process in a blender until blended and return to the saucepan. Add the milk and half-and-half. Cook until heated through; do not boil. Add salt and white pepper. Ladle into soup bowls. Dot with the butter and sprinkle with the parsley and paprika.

Serves 4

Reach high, for stars lie hidden in your soul. Dream deep, for
every dream precedes the goal.

—PAMELA VAULL STARR

Tangy Tomato Bisque

6 tablespoons unsalted butter
1/2 cup chopped onion
1 1/2 teaspoons minced fresh dill weed
2 pounds tomatoes, chopped
4 cups chicken broth
2 tablespoons unsalted butter

2 tablespoons all-purpose flour
1 1/4 cups heavy cream
2/3 cup half-and-half
1/4 cup fresh flat-leaf parsley, minced
1/4 cup local honey
Salt and pepper to taste

Melt 6 tablespoons butter in a large stockpot over medium heat. Add the onion and 1 1/2 teaspoons dill weed and sauté for 5 minutes or until the onion is translucent. Add the tomatoes and broth. Bring to a simmer and remove from the heat.

Melt 2 tablespoons butter in a small saucepan over medium heat. Add the flour. Cook for 3 minutes, stirring constantly with a wooden spoon. Do not brown. Add the cream and half-and-half. Bring to a boil, stirring occasionally. Reduce the heat to medium-low and simmer for 15 minutes. Stir in the parsley and honey. Remove from the heat.

Purée the cream mixture with the tomato mixture in batches in a food processor or blender, pouring each batch into a stockpot. Heat over low heat until heated through. Sprinkle with salt and pepper. Ladle into warm shallow soup bowls and garnish with additional dill weed.

Serves 6 to 8

In order to succeed, we must first believe that we can.

—MICHAEL KORDA

Old-Fashioned Vegetable Soup

2 pounds soup meat of choice
3 quarts water
4 cabbage leaves, shredded
5 sprigs of parsley
2 small onions, chopped
1 cup green beans
2 carrots, peeled and chopped
1 turnip, chopped
1 potato, chopped
1 cup fresh or frozen whole kernel corn
1/2 cup chopped celery
1 (20-ounce) can stewed tomatoes
Salt and pepper to taste
Brown sugar to taste

Combine the meat, water, cabbage, parsley, onions, green beans, carrots, turnip, potato, corn, celery and tomatoes in a stockpot. Cover and bring to a boil. Reduce the heat and simmer for 2 hours, skimming off the top as needed. Add salt, pepper and brown sugar, if desired. Ladle into soup bowls.

Serves 8

When nothing is sure, everything is possible!
—MARGARET DRABBLE

Salads

Cooking Up Fun With Kids

No-Cook Play-Dough

2 cups all-purpose flour
1 cup salt
Water
Food coloring or tempera paint
2 tablespoons vegetable oil (optional)

Mix the flour and salt together in a bowl. Add enough water
to make of a dough consistency.

Tint the dough with food coloring. Add the oil and mix well.

NOTE: Omit the oil if you want your artwork to harden as it dries.

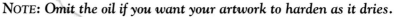

Berry-licious Chicken Salad

Candied Walnuts
1 egg white
10 ounces walnuts, chopped
2/3 cup packed brown sugar

Berry Champagne Vinaigrette
1 small purple onion,
   cut into quarters
1 small garlic clove
1 tablespoon Creole mustard
2 tablespoons sugar
1/8 teaspoon salt
Dash of white pepper
1/2 cup Champagne vinegar

1/3 cup blackberries, rinsed
11/2 cups extra-virgin olive oil

Salad
1 pound mixed baby greens
11/4 pounds boneless skinless chicken
   breasts, cooked and julienned
11/2 cups crumbled blue cheese
   (about 6 ounces)
Salt and freshly ground pepper to taste
1 cup raspberries, rinsed
1 cup blackberries, rinsed
1 cup strawberries, rinsed and
   cut into halves

To prepare the walnuts, whisk the egg white in a mixing bowl until foamy and no liquid remains. Fold in the walnuts and brown sugar and toss gently to coat evenly. Arrange the walnuts separately on a baking sheet sprayed with nonstick cooking spray. Bake at 325 degrees for 12 to 14 minutes or until golden brown. Remove the walnuts with a spatula to a plate to cool.

To prepare the vinaigrette, process the onion and garlic in a blender until minced. Add the mustard, sugar, salt, pepper, vinegar, blackberries and 1/2 cup of the candied walnuts and process until combined. Add the olive oil in a thin steady stream, processing constantly until emulsified. Adjust the seasonings to taste.

To prepare the salad, combine the greens, chicken, blue cheese and 2 cups of the candied walnuts in a large bowl. Drizzle about 1 cup of the vinaigrette over the salad and toss gently to coat. Season with salt and pepper. Add two-thirds of the raspberries, two-thirds of the blackberries and two-thirds of the strawberries and toss gently to mix. Serve and sprinkle with the remaining raspberries, blackberries and strawberries. (Note: The candied walnuts can be prepared 2 days ahead and stored in an airtight container.)

Serves 6 to 12

Children will not remember you for the material things you provided but for the feeling that you cherished them.

—RICHARD L. EVANS

The Peach Festival Chicken Salad

Ginger Cinnamon Dressing

6 tablespoons mayonnaise
6 tablespoons sour cream
3/4 teaspoon lemon juice
1/2 teaspoon dried tarragon, or to taste
1/8 teaspoon salt
1/8 teaspoon ginger
1/8 teaspoon cinnamon

Salad

8 cups Bibb lettuce, torn
2 cups chopped cooked chicken
2 cups fresh peaches, peeled and sliced (1 1/4 pounds)
1/2 cup raisins
Torn Bibb lettuce leaves to taste
2 tablespoons chopped fresh chives

To prepare the dressing, combine the mayonnaise, sour cream, lemon juice, tarragon, salt, ginger and cinnamon in a bowl and mix well.

To prepare the salad, combine 8 cups Bibb lettuce, the chicken, peaches and raisins in a bowl. Add the desired amount of dressing and toss to coat. Line four salad plates with torn Bibb lettuce leaves. Spoon 2 cups of the salad onto each of the prepared plates. Sprinkle with the chives and serve immediately.

Serves 4

*A child's life is like a piece of paper on which
every person leaves a mark.*
—CHINESE PROVERB

Calcasieu Chicken Salad with Hearts of Artichokes and Palm in Creole Mayonnaise

Creole Mayonnaise

2 cups premium mayonnaise

1/2 cup plus 2 tablespoons
   Creole mustard

Creole seasoning to taste

Creole red sauce to taste

1 to 1 1/2 tablespoons fresh lemon
   juice, or to taste

Salad

2 (6-ounce) jars marinated
   artichoke hearts

5 chicken breasts

White wine or water for poaching

1 (7- to 8-ounce) can hearts of palm,
   drained and sliced

Salad greens (optional)

To prepare the mayonnaise, combine the mayonnaise, Creole mustard, Creole seasoning, red sauce and lemon juice in a bowl and mix well.

To prepare the salad, drain the artichoke hearts, reserving the marinade. Combine the Creole Mayonnaise and the reserved marinade in a bowl and mix well. Chill in the refrigerator. Place the chicken in a skillet or saucepan with just enough wine to cover. Bring to a boil over medium heat and reduce the heat. Simmer for 12 minutes or until the chicken is cooked through. Remove the chicken with a slotted spoon and drain well. Cool to room temperature. Cut the chicken into bite-size pieces, discarding the skin and bones. Combine the chicken, drained artichoke hearts, hearts of palm and the mayonnaise mixture in a bowl and mix well. Serve over a bed of salad greens and garnish with chopped pecans and chopped fresh parsley.

(Note: Double or triple the recipe for Creole Mayonnaise. Use 2 1/2 to 2 3/4 cups of the mayonnaise in the salad and store the excess in an airtight container in the refrigerator to use on Creole sandwiches. The salad can be chilled for 8 to 10 hours before serving. Garnish just before serving.)

Serves 6 to 8

The race is not always to the swift, but to those who keep on running.

—ANONYMOUS

"Tooloulou" (Crab) Salad with Avocado

Salsa

1/2 cup red bell pepper, finely chopped
2 plum tomatoes, chopped
2 scallions, thinly sliced diagonally
1 garlic clove, minced
2 tablespoons cilantro, coarsely chopped
2 teaspoons minced jalapeño chiles
1/4 teaspoon salt
Pinch of pepper

Salad

2 avocados, finely chopped
3 tablespoons lime juice
Salt and freshly ground pepper to taste
2 1/2 cups fresh lump crab meat
1/4 cup sour cream

To prepare the salsa, combine the bell pepper, tomatoes, scallions, garlic, cilantro, jalapeño chiles, salt and a pinch of pepper in a bowl and toss to mix. Let stand at room temperature for 20 minutes.

To prepare the salad, combine the avocados, lime juice, salt and pepper to taste in a bowl and toss to coat. Layer 1/4 cup of the salsa, 5 tablespoons of the crab meat and 2 tablespoons of the avocado mixture in each of eight 6-ounce parfait glasses or Champagne flutes. Spoon 1 1/2 teaspoons sour cream on top of each. Garnish each with some of the remaining salsa.

Serves 8

*Careful grooming may take twenty years off a woman's
age, but it won't fool a long flight of stairs.*

—ANONYMOUS

Shrimp Salad with Lime and Cilantro Vinaigrette

Lime and Cilantro Vinaigrette

1/3 cup seasoned rice wine vinegar
1/4 cup fresh lime juice
1 garlic clove, finely chopped
1 teaspoon puréed chipotle chiles in
   adobo sauce
2 tablespoons local honey
1/2 teaspoon salt
3/4 cup canola oil
1 cup chopped fresh cilantro stems
   and leaves

Salad

3 ears of corn, shucked and grilled
   or boiled
2 pounds large shrimp, cooked and
   peeled (about 36)
1/2 cup chopped tomatoes
1 pound mixed baby salad greens
2 cups (8 ounces) shredded Jack cheese
1/2 cup chopped roasted red bell pepper
Salt and pepper to taste
3/4 cup toasted salted pumpkin seeds
   or nuts

To prepare the vinaigrette, process the vinegar, lime juice, garlic, chipotle chiles, honey and salt in a blender until smooth. Add the canola oil in a thin steady stream, processing constantly until emulsified. Add the cilantro and pulse to combine. Adjust the seasonings to taste and set aside.

To prepare the salad, cut the corn kernels from the ears of corn into a large bowl. Add the shrimp, tomatoes, salad greens, cheese and bell pepper. Drizzle with the vinaigrette and toss gently to coat. Season with salt and pepper. Sprinkle with the pumpkin seeds. Garnish with lime wedges. (*Note: To roast bell peppers and corn, place on a grill rack over medium-high heat. Roast for 2 to 3 minutes per side or until each side of the bell pepper has blistered and blackened and the corn is tender. Remove from the grill rack and place in a bowl. Cover tightly with plastic wrap and let cool for 15 minutes. Uncover and peel away the skin from the bell pepper. Cut the bell pepper into slices lengthwise and remove the stems, seeds and ribs. Cut the corn kernels from the cob into a bowl. Three ears of corn should yield about 2 cups roasted whole kernel corn.*)

Serves 6

*We should never permit ourselves to do anything that we are
not willing to see our children do.*

—BRIGHAM YOUNG

Tomato, Cucumber and Grilled Bread Salad with Fresh Basil

8 ounces French bread, cut into 3/4-inch-thick slices
2 tablespoons extra-virgin olive oil
4 cups coarsely chopped heirloom tomatoes
    (about 3 large tomatoes)
2 cups coarsely chopped peeled cucumbers
1/4 cup lightly packed fresh basil, torn into small pieces
1 tablespoon red wine vinegar, or to taste
1/4 cup extra-virgin olive oil
Salt and pepper to taste

Brush the bread on both sides with 2 tablespoons olive oil. Place on a grill rack. Grill over medium heat for 3 to 4 minutes or until lightly charred on both sides. Let cool slightly and cut into cubes of the desired size. Toss the bread cubes with the tomatoes, cucumbers and basil in a large bowl. Drizzle with the vinegar and 1/4 cup olive oil. Season with salt and pepper. Toss to combine and serve.

Serves 4

Belief is truth in the mind; faith is a fire in the heart.
—JOHN FISCHER

Tortellini Salad with Feta Cheese

1/2 cup olive oil
1/2 cup white wine vinegar
1/2 cup chopped green onions
2 garlic cloves, chopped
2 to 3 (12-ounce) packages frozen cheese tortellini, cooked
2 (8-ounce) cans artichoke hearts, drained and chopped
2 tomatoes, chopped
6 ounces feta cheese, crumbled
1 (4-ounce) can chopped black olives
1 tablespoon basil
1 tablespoon dried dill weed
1 cup walnuts, chopped

Whisk the olive oil, vinegar, green onions and garlic in a bowl. Combine the tortellini, artichoke hearts, tomatoes, cheese, olives, basil, dill weed and walnuts in a bowl. Add the dressing and toss gently. Chill, covered, for 8 to 10 hours. Serve chilled. (*Note: You may use store-bought vinaigrette and 1/2 cup chopped green onions.*)

Serves 6 to 8

A friend may well be reckoned the masterpiece of Nature.
—RALPH WALDO EMERSON

Asparagus Salad with Tangerine Dressing

Tangerine Dressing

1/3 cup fresh tangerine juice or orange juice
1 1/2 teaspoons grated tangerine zest or orange zest
1 1/2 teaspoons Oriental sesame oil
3/4 teaspoon minced peeled fresh ginger
2 teaspoons rice vinegar
1 garlic clove, pressed

Salad

1 pound asparagus, trimmed
1 teaspoon olive oil
Salt and pepper to taste
2 tablespoons minced chives
2 tablespoons peanuts, finely chopped

To prepare the dressing, whisk the tangerine juice, tangerine zest, sesame oil, ginger, vinegar and garlic in a bowl and set aside.

To prepare the salad, place the asparagus in a bowl and cover with water. Let stand for 15 minutes; drain. Arrange the asparagus in a single layer in a 9×13-inch baking pan. Drizzle with the olive oil. Bake at 450 degrees for 10 minutes or until tender-crisp, turning occasionally. Remove to a platter to cool. Season with salt and pepper. Sprinkle with the chives and peanuts. Serve with the dressing to taste. (*Note: You will need two large tangerines or small oranges for the juice and zest.*)

Serves 8

In America, there are two classes of travel,
first class and with children.

—ROBERT BENCHLEY

Spring Salad with Louisiana Blackberries, Figs and Local Honey Dressing

Local Honey Dressing

2 teaspoons sherry vinegar
1/2 teaspoon local honey
Salt and freshly cracked pepper to taste
2 tablespoons extra-virgin olive oil

Salad

2 cups spring salad mix
8 figs
Fresh blackberries
Chopped honey roasted nuts to taste

To prepare the dressing, mix the vinegar, honey, salt and pepper in a bowl with a fork. Add the olive oil and blend until emulsified.

To prepare the salad, arrange the salad mix on individual serving plates. Rinse the figs and pat dry. Cut into quarters and arrange on the salad mix. Top with the blackberries. Drizzle the dressing over the salads and sprinkle with the nuts.

Serves 4

Instill great values in your children today, and your grandchildren will prosper tomorrow.

—CHRISTY BORGELD

Endive and Pear Salad

$1/2$ cup walnuts, coarsely chopped
1 tablespoon water
1 tablespoon sugar
Creole seasoning to taste
$1^1/2$ tablespoons extra-virgin olive oil
$1^1/2$ tablespoons vegetable oil
1 tablespoon balsamic vinegar
Salt and freshly cracked pepper to taste
1 bunch watercress, stems trimmed
2 heads Belgium endive, sliced crosswise
1 pear, cut into halves and thinly sliced

Combine the walnuts, water, sugar and Creole seasoning in a small skillet. Cook over medium heat for 4 minutes or until the water evaporates and the walnuts are dry and golden brown, stirring constantly. Remove from the heat to cool.

Whisk the olive oil, vegetable oil and vinegar in a small bowl until blended. Season with salt and pepper. Combine the watercress, endive and pear in a large bowl. Add the dressing and toss to coat. Sprinkle with the walnuts.

Serves 6

You might be a Cajun if…You refer to Louisiana winters as "gumbo weather."

—ANONYMOUS

Garden District Salad

8 ounces fresh asparagus, trimmed
1 garlic clove, minced
1 tablespoon brown sugar
2 tablespoons extra-virgin olive oil
2 tablespoons white wine vinegar
1 tablespoon water
1 teaspoon spicy Creole mustard
1/4 teaspoon dried rubbed sage
1/4 teaspoon salt
1/4 teaspoon freshly cracked pepper

10 grape tomatoes, cut into halves
1 (19-ounce) can cannellini beans,
 drained and rinsed
1/4 cup chopped red onion
2 teaspoons drained capers
1 (5-ounce) package gourmet mixed
 salad greens
1 tablespoon shredded
 Parmesan cheese

Snap off the tough ends of the asparagus. Arrange the asparagus in a steamer basket over boiling water in a saucepan. Cover and steam for 2 to 4 minutes or until the asparagus is tender-crisp. Plunge the asparagus into ice water to stop the cooking process; drain. Cut the asparagus into 1-inch pieces. Chill until needed.

Whisk the garlic, brown sugar, olive oil, vinegar, 1 tablespoon water, the Creole mustard, sage, salt and pepper in a medium bowl. Add the asparagus, tomatoes, beans, onion and capers and toss to coat. Chill, covered, for 1 hour.

Spoon the asparagus mixture over the salad greens on a serving plate. Sprinkle with the cheese.

Serves 6

Pick the flower when it is ready to be picked.
—CHINESE PROVERB

Tater 'N Corn Salad

2 pounds small skinned white potatoes
Salt to taste
1/2 cup buttermilk
1/4 cup mayonnaise
1 tablespoon fresh lemon juice
1/2 teaspoon ground cumin
Creole seasoning to taste
1 cup cooked whole kernel corn
1/2 cup finely chopped yellow onion
1 (14-ounce) can hearts of palm, drained and
    cut into 1/3-inch rounds
2 plum tomatoes, seeded and chopped
1/2 cup fresh cilantro, chopped
Tabasco sauce to taste
1 avocado, peeled and chopped

Cook the potatoes in boiling salted water in a large saucepan for 20 minutes or until tender; drain and cool. Cut the potatoes into 1 1/2-inch cubes. Whisk the buttermilk, mayonnaise, lemon juice, cumin and Creole seasoning in a medium bowl. Combine the potatoes, corn, onion, hearts of palm, tomatoes and cilantro in a large bowl. Drizzle with the dressing and toss to coat. Season with Creole seasoning and Tabasco sauce. Stir in the avocado gently and serve.

Serves 6

*Affirming words from moms and dads are like light switches.
Speak a word of affirmation at the right moment in a child's life and
it's like lighting up a whole roomful of possibilities.*

—GARY SMALLEY

Yam-Good Potato Salad

2 pounds red-skinned sweet potatoes or yams,
    peeled and cut into 1/2-inch cubes
1/4 cup rice vinegar
1/4 cup soy sauce
3 tablespoons mayonnaise
4 teaspoons minced peeled fresh ginger
4 teaspoons toasted sesame oil
4 garlic cloves, minced
1 tablespoon peanut butter
2 teaspoons chili-garlic sauce
1 1/2 teaspoons light brown sugar
1 1/2 cups blanched sugar snap peas, cut crosswise
    into 1/2-inch pieces
1 cup thinly sliced green onions
Salt and pepper to taste
1/2 cup dry-roasted peanuts, coarsely chopped

Place enough water in a large saucepan to reach a depth of 1/2 inch. Bring to a boil. Add the sweet potatoes. Cook for 8 to 10 minutes or until tender. Do not overcook. Drain the sweet potatoes. Whisk the vinegar, soy sauce, mayonnaise, ginger, sesame oil, garlic, peanut butter, chili-garlic sauce and brown sugar in a large bowl until blended. Add the sweet potatoes, peas, green onions, salt and pepper and toss to mix. Spoon into a serving bowl. Sprinkle with the peanuts and serve. (Note: This salad can be made 4 hours ahead and stored, covered, in the refrigerator.)

Serves 6 to 8

Keep true to the dreams of thy youth.

—JOHAN FRIEDRICH VON SCHILLER

"Grand Prix" Coleslaw with Carrots and Apples

1/3 cup pineapple juice
1/4 cup sugar
1/4 cup olive oil
1/4 cup lemon juice or lime juice
1/4 cup rice wine vinegar
1/2 teaspoon salt
1/2 teaspoon pepper
1/8 teaspoon Louisiana hot pepper sauce
1 large head red cabbage, finely shredded
1 small Granny Smith apple, chopped
1 large carrot, shredded
1 small sweet onion, minced
5 or 6 slices bacon, cooked and crumbled

Whisk the pineapple juice, sugar, olive oil, lemon juice, vinegar, salt, pepper and hot pepper sauce in a large bowl until the sugar dissolves. Add the cabbage, apple, carrot and onion and toss to coat. Chill, covered, for 1 hour or longer. Sprinkle with the bacon just before serving.

Serves 8

I am not bound to win, but I am bound to be true. I am not bound to succeed, but to live up what light I have.

—ABRAHAM LINCOLN

Spicy Puh-Kawn Slaw

Spicy Dressing
4 cups (32 ounces) nonfat
    vegetable stock
2 tablespoons cornstarch
1 teaspoon cumin seeds
1 jalapeño chile, seeded and
    finely chopped
1 garlic clove
1/2 shallot, chopped
1/2 cup fresh cilantro, chopped
1/4 cup sweet chili sauce
1/4 cup apple cider

1/2 teaspoon ground cumin
1/4 teaspoon pepper

Chili Pecans
1/4 cup pecan pieces
1/2 teaspoon chili powder
1 tablespoon olive oil

Slaw
4 ounces red cabbage, shredded
4 ounces green cabbage, shredded
1 each small green, red and yellow
    bell pepper, thinly sliced

To prepare the dressing, blend 1/2 cup of the stock with the cornstarch in a glass measure. Bring the remaining 3 1/2 cups stock to a boil in a medium saucepan over high heat. Reduce the heat to a simmer. Whisk in the cornstarch mixture gradually. Cook until the mixture is the consistency of olive oil and clings to the back of a spoon, stirring constantly. Remove from the heat to cool, skimming off and discarding any film that forms on the top. Sauté the cumin seeds in a dry sauté pan over medium-high heat for 1 minute or until the aroma of the seeds is released. Blend 1/4 cup of the stock mixture with the cumin seeds in a blender. Add the jalapeño chile, garlic, shallot, cilantro, chili sauce, apple cider, cumin and pepper and blend until smooth. Reserve the remaining stock mixture for another purpose; store in the refrigerator or freezer.

To prepare the pecans, combine the pecans, chili powder and olive oil in a bowl and toss to coat. Spread in a single layer on a baking sheet. Bake at 350 degrees for 3 to 4 minutes or until the aroma of the chili powder is released.

To prepare the slaw, combine the red cabbage, green cabbage and bell peppers in a large bowl. Add the dressing and pecans and toss to coat. Chill, covered, in the refrigerator until serving time.

Serves 4

When you get to the end of your rope tie a knot and hang on.
—FRANKLIN DELANO ROOSEVELT

Cold Rice Salad

1/2 cup wild rice, cooked and chilled
1/2 cup brown rice, cooked and chilled
1/2 cup white rice, cooked and chilled
1 cup slivered almonds
3 green onions, chopped
4 ribs celery, chopped
1/2 cup chopped cucumber
2 navel oranges, peeled and chopped
1 teaspoon Dijon mustard
1/2 cup olive oil
1/4 cup red wine vinegar
2 tablespoons mayonnaise
1/8 teaspoon sugar
Salt and pepper to taste

Combine the wild rice, brown rice and white rice in a bowl and mix well. Add the almonds, green onions, celery, cucumber and oranges and toss lightly. Whisk the Dijon mustard, olive oil, vinegar, mayonnaise, sugar, salt and pepper in a bowl until blended. Pour over the rice mixture and toss lightly. Chill, covered, in the refrigerator. Bring to room temperature before serving.

Serves 6

Pleasure in the job puts perfection in the work.
—ARISTOTLE

Entrées

Cooking Up Fun With Kids

PAPIER-MÂCHÉ

Chicken wire, rolled newspaper or balloon
1 part liquid starch
1 part cold water
Newspapers

Shape chicken wire, rolled newspaper or a balloon into the desired
shape. Mix equal parts liquid starch and cold water in a bowl.
Tear newspapers into strips.

Dip the newspaper strips one at a time into the starch mixture
and apply to the form. Continue until the entire form is covered with
several thicknesses of the wet newspaper strips. Let stand until dry.
Decorate as desired.

NOTE: *For papier-mâché masks, blow up a balloon and cover with
newspaper strips dipped in the glue mixture. Let stand until dry.
Pop the balloon and cut the hardened shell into halves. Decorate the
masks by gluing three-dimensional objects on them.*

Spud 'n Tails Stuffed Bell Peppers

4 large baking potatoes
  (about 3¹/2 to 4 pounds)
4 large red bell peppers
1 pound crawfish tails, cooked,
  peeled and coarsely chopped
2 tablespoons butter
Creole seasoning to taste
2 cups sour cream

¹/2 cup (2 ounces) shredded
  Gouda cheese
¹/4 cup sliced green onions
¹/4 cup (¹/2 stick) butter
3 tablespoons fresh flat-leaf
  parsley, chopped
Salt and pepper to taste
¹/4 teaspoon paprika

Pierce each potato three or four times with a fork and place directly on an oven rack. Bake at 450 degrees for 1¹/2 hours. Let cool for 15 minutes. Cut the bell peppers into halves lengthwise, cutting through the stems and keeping intact. Discard the seeds and membranes. Rinse the bell pepper halves and pat dry. Sauté the crawfish tails in 2 tablespoons butter in a skillet. Season with Creole seasoning. Remove with a slotted spoon to a plate and coarsely chop.

Cut the baked potatoes into halves. Scoop the pulp into a large bowl, discarding the shells. Add the sour cream, cheese, green onions, ¹/4 cup butter, the parsley, salt and pepper and mash with a fork or potato masher. Add the crawfish tails and mix gently. Spoon evenly into the bell pepper halves. Sprinkle with the paprika. Place on a grill rack. Grill, covered with the grill lid, over medium-high heat (350 to 400 degrees) for 18 minutes or until the bell peppers are blistered and the potato mixture bubbles around the edges. Serve immediately. (Note: Do not microwave the potatoes; the results are not as good. Yellow or green bell peppers may be used instead of the red bell peppers. Your favorite cheese may be used instead of the Gouda cheese.)

Serves 8

Life affords no greater responsibility, no greater privilege, than the raising of the next generation.

—C. Everet Koop, M.D.

Classy Country Club Crawfish
Over Cheese Ravioli

1/4 cup (1/2 stick) butter
2 tablespoons all-purpose flour
1 onion, minced
2 garlic cloves, minced
2 tablespoons parsley, minced
2 tablespoons green onions, minced
1 pound cooked crawfish tails
1/2 cup white wine
1 cup heavy cream
Creole seasoning to taste
1 (12-ounce) package frozen cheese ravioli
Freshly grated Parmesan cheese to taste
Finely chopped fresh parsley

Melt the butter in a skillet. Stir in the flour. Cook the mixture slightly, stirring constantly. Add the onion, garlic, 2 tablespoons parsley and the green onions. Cook until the vegetables are soft. Add the crawfish tails. Cook over low heat for 10 minutes. Add the wine and bring to a simmer. Add the cream gradually, stirring constantly. Return to a simmer; do not boil or the mixture will curdle. Sprinkle with Creole seasoning.

Prepare the ravioli using the package directions. Place in a serving bowl. Spoon the crawfish mixture over the ravioli. Sprinkle with the cheese and finely chopped parsley.

Serves 4

*If you want children to keep their feet on the ground, put
some responsibility on their shoulders.*

—ABIGAIL VAN BUREN

Crawfish Jambalaya

1 cup uncooked long grain rice
2 cups chicken broth
1/4 cup (1/2 stick) butter
1 onion, chopped
1/2 cup chopped green bell pepper
1/2 cup chopped celery
4 garlic cloves, minced
1 (14-ounce) can stewed tomatoes
1 teaspoon Cajun seasoning
1 pound frozen crawfish tails, thawed, rinsed and drained
1 cup chopped green onions
1/8 teaspoon pepper

Cook the rice using the package directions, substituting the broth for the water. Melt the butter in a Dutch oven over medium-high heat. Add the onion, bell pepper and celery. Sauté for 8 minutes or until the vegetables are tender. Add the garlic. Sauté for 1 minute. Stir in the tomatoes and Cajun seasoning. Reduce the heat to low and simmer for 15 to 20 minutes. Add the crawfish tails. Cook for 5 minutes. Stir in the green onions, cooked rice and pepper. Garnish with additional chopped green onions.

Serves 4 to 6

We give nothing so freely as advice.
—FRANCOIS DE LA ROCHEFOUCAULD

Crab Sandwich

3 tablespoons butter
2 tablespoons all-purpose flour
1 1/2 cups light cream
Creole seasoning to taste
Louisiana hot pepper sauce to taste
1/2 cup (2 ounces) shredded Swiss cheese
2 tablespoons freshly grated Parmesan cheese
4 English muffins
Butter for spreading
1 pound crab meat
8 slices Cheddar cheese
2 avocados, thinly sliced

Melt 3 tablespoons butter in a saucepan over medium heat. Stir in the flour until blended. Add the cream, Creole seasoning, hot pepper sauce, Swiss cheese and Parmesan cheese. Cook until the cheeses melt, stirring constantly.

Split the English muffins with a fork. Butter the cut sides and place on a baking sheet. Bake at 350 degrees until toasted. Layer a spoonful of the sauce, the crab meat, Cheddar cheese and another spoonful of the sauce on each muffin half. Bake until the Cheddar cheese melts and is brown. Top each with the avocados and serve hot.

Serves 4

They will say that you are on the wrong road if it is your own.
—ANTONIO PORCHIA

Traditional Oyster Casserole

2 tablespoons butter
3 green onions, finely chopped
1 red bell pepper, chopped
8 ounces fresh mushrooms, sliced
2 quarts oysters, drained
2 tablespoons butter
1/4 cup all-purpose flour
1 cup heavy cream

1/4 cup (1 ounce) freshly grated
    Parmesan cheese
Freshly grated nutmeg to taste
1/2 teaspoon paprika
Creole seasoning to taste
1/2 cup cracker crumbs
1/4 cup (1/2 stick) butter

Melt 2 tablespoons butter in a large sauté pan. Add the green onions and bell pepper. Sauté for 5 minutes or until the green onions are soft. Add the mushrooms and oysters. Sauté for 5 minutes.

Melt 2 tablespoons butter in a saucepan. Stir in the flour until smooth. Add the cream and cook until the mixture boils and is thick, stirring constantly. Stir in the cheese. Stir the sauce into the oyster mixture. Add the nutmeg, paprika and Creole seasoning. (The casserole may be made ahead up to this point and chilled, covered, for 8 to 10 hours. Return to a simmer before proceeding.)

Spoon the mixture into a greased 9×13-inch baking dish. Top with the cracker crumbs and dot with 1/4 cup butter. Broil for 10 minutes or until brown and bubbly.

Serves 10 to 12

You might be from Louisiana if... The four seasons in your year are: crawfish, shrimp, crab, and King Cake.

—ANONYMOUS

Corn-Dusted Scallops with Pineapple-Mango Salsa

Pineapple-Mango Salsa

1 cup chopped fresh pineapple
1 cup chopped mango
1 cup chopped yellow and red
   bell peppers
2/3 cup chopped kiwifruit
1/2 cup chopped red onion
1/4 cup fresh cilantro
1 teaspoon chopped serrano chile or
   mild jalapeño chile
Salt and white pepper to taste

Coconut Rice

2 cups uncooked rice
2 cups coconut milk
1 cup water
2 tablespoons butter
Salt to taste

Scallops

1 tablespoon olive oil
2 pounds sea scallops
3 cups yellow cornmeal
Creole seasoning to taste
Chopped chives to taste

To prepare the salsa, combine the pineapple, mango, bell peppers, kiwifruit, onion, cilantro, serrano chile, salt and white pepper in a medium bowl and toss to mix.

To prepare the rice, rinse the rice once or twice to remove the excess starch; drain. Combine the drained rice, coconut milk, water, butter and salt in a saucepan. Bring to a boil over medium heat, stirring frequently. Cook until the water is reduced slightly. Reduce the heat. Cover tightly with a lid and simmer for 20 minutes.

To prepare the scallops, heat the olive oil in a large nonstick skillet over medium-high heat. Dust the scallops with a mixture of the cornmeal and Creole seasoning. Cook for 3 minutes on each side or until tender.

To serve, spoon the scallops and salsa over the coconut rice. Sprinkle with the chives. (Note: Any fruit combination will work when preparing the salsa. The salsa is best served right away, but it can be made 1 day in advance and stored in the refrigerator.)

Serves 4

One thing worse than being a quitter—is being afraid to make a start.

—ANONYMOUS

Spicy Grits with Shrimp

3 cups water
1 cup whipping cream
$1/4$ cup ($1/2$ stick) butter
Salt to taste
1 cup quick-cooking grits
1 pound fresh shrimp, cooked, peeled and deveined
1 cup (4 ounces) shredded sharp Cheddar cheese or
    Pepper Jack Cheddar cheese
Garlic powder to taste
Butter to taste
Louisiana hot pepper sauce to taste
Shredded Pepper Jack cheese (optional)
Finely chopped green onions (optional)

Bring the water, cream, $1/4$ cup butter and salt to a boil in a large saucepan over medium-high heat. Reduce the heat to medium. Stir in the grits. Cook for 7 to 8 minutes or until the mixture is smooth, stirring constantly. Stir in the shrimp, Cheddar cheese and garlic powder. Stir in butter to taste and hot pepper sauce. Cook for 1 to 2 minutes or until heated through. Sprinkle with Pepper Jack cheese and green onions.

Serves 4

Children have more need of models than of critics.
—CAROLYN COATS

Shrimp and Catfish Court Bouillon

2 yellow onions, chopped
1 green bell pepper, chopped
2 garlic cloves, chopped
1 tablespoon salt
1 tablespoon black pepper
1 tablespoon cayenne pepper
1 tablespoon vegetable oil
3 pounds catfish, cut up

2 tablespoons all-purpose flour
1 (8-ounce) can tomato sauce
1 cup water
2 pounds shrimp, peeled and deveined
1 bunch green onion tops, chopped
1 bunch parsley, chopped
Hot cooked rice

Mix the onions, bell pepper and garlic in a bowl and set aside. Mix the salt, black pepper and cayenne pepper in a small bowl and set aside. Heat the oil in a cast-iron or Magnalite Dutch oven over medium-low heat. Alternate layers of the vegetable mixture, fish, seasoning mixture, flour, tomato sauce and water in the Dutch oven until all the ingredients are used. Simmer, covered, over low heat for 30 minutes. Add the shrimp. Simmer for 15 minutes. Add the green onions and parsley. Cook for 5 minutes. Serve over hot cooked rice.

Serves 6

It is a wise father that knows his own child.
—WILLIAM SHAKESPEARE

Catfish with Spicy Strawberry Sauce

2 pounds catfish fillets
Salt and pepper to taste
2 ounces Louisiana hot pepper sauce
1 1/2 cups strawberry preserves
1/2 cup red wine vinegar
1 tablespoon soy sauce
1/4 cup seafood cocktail sauce
1 garlic clove, minced
2 teaspoons horseradish
3/4 cup cornmeal
3/4 cup all-purpose flour
1/2 cup safflower oil

Place the fish in a large shallow dish. Sprinkle with salt, pepper and hot pepper sauce. Chill, covered, for 1 hour.

Combine the preserves, vinegar, soy sauce, cocktail sauce, garlic and horseradish in a small saucepan. Simmer over low heat, stirring occasionally.

Mix the cornmeal and flour in a shallow dish. Drain the fish and dredge in the cornmeal mixture, coating all sides. Heat the oil in a heavy skillet over medium heat. Add the fish to the hot oil and sauté until brown on both sides. Remove to paper towels to drain. Keep warm.

Spoon 1/4 cup of the sauce onto each serving plate. Top each with a fish fillet. Garnish with sliced strawberries and sprigs of fresh parsley.

Serves 5

Living consciously involves being genuine. It involves listening and responding to others honestly and openly. It involves being in the moment.

—SIDNEY POITIER

Fillets of Sole Bonne Femme

2 shallots, chopped
2 tablespoons butter
2 1/2 pounds sole fillets
8 mushrooms, sliced
1/2 teaspoon salt
1/8 teaspoon freshly cracked pepper
1 cup dry white wine
1 garlic clove, minced
1 tablespoon fresh parsley, chopped
2 tablespoons butter
1 1/2 teaspoons all-purpose flour

Sauté the shallots in 2 tablespoons butter in a large skillet for 2 minutes. Rinse the fish and pat dry. Arrange the fish over the shallots. Top with the mushrooms and season with salt and pepper. Add the wine and garlic. Bring to a boil and reduce the heat. Simmer, covered, for 10 minutes. Add the parsley. Cook for 5 minutes or until the fish flakes easily. Drain well, reserving 1 cup of the cooking liquid. Place the fish and mushrooms in an 8×12-inch baking pan.

Melt 2 tablespoons butter in a skillet. Stir in the flour. Add the reserved liquid gradually, stirring constantly. Cook over medium heat until thickened, stirring constantly. Pour over the fish. Broil for 3 to 5 minutes or until the tops are golden brown.

Serves 6

There is nothing that can help you understand your beliefs more than trying to explain them to an inquisitive child.

—FRANK A. CLARK

Pan-Fried Tilapia

4 tilapia fillets
Olive oil for drizzling
Salt and black pepper to taste
1 tablespoon minced garlic
All-purpose flour
1/2 cup olive oil
1/4 cup chopped green onions
2 tablespoons minced garlic
Pinch of red pepper flakes
1 tablespoon lemon zest
1 cup half-and-half
Juice of 1 lemon

Drizzle the fish with olive oil. Sprinkle with salt, black pepper and 1 tablespoon garlic and rub into the fish. Season the flour with salt and black pepper. Heat 1/2 cup olive in a skillet. Dredge the fish in the flour mixture and shake off the excess. Add the fish to the hot olive oil and cook for 3 minutes on each side or until golden brown. Remove the fish to a platter and keep warm.

Drain the skillet, reserving 2 tablespoons of the liquid. Add the green onions, 2 tablespoons garlic, the red pepper flakes and lemon zest and sauté for 3 minutes or until tender. Add the half-and-half. Bring to a boil and reduce the heat. Simmer for 15 minutes. Stir in the lemon juice.

Plate the fish and serve the sauce on the side or over the fish.

Serves 2 to 4

Success is a journey, not a destination.

—BEN SWEETLAND

Fish Tacos

Fruit Salsa
Chopped mango
1 firm banana, chopped
2 scallions, chopped
3 tablespoons fresh cilantro, chopped
1 or 2 jalapeño chiles, seeded
  and minced

Tacos
2 tablespoons fresh lemon juice
2 or 3 teaspoons olive oil
1 teaspoon ground allspice

1 teaspoon chili powder
1/2 teaspoon ground cloves
2 or 3 garlic cloves, minced
1 or 2 teaspoons grated lemon zest or
  lime zest
1 pound fresh fish fillets, such as
  mahi mahi or tilapia
4 tortillas
Shredded lettuce
Shredded red cabbage
Thinly sliced red onion

To prepare the salsa, combine the mango, banana, scallions, cilantro and jalapeño chiles in a small bowl and toss to mix.

To prepare the tacos, combine the lemon juice, olive oil, allspice, chili powder, cloves, garlic and lemon zest in a bowl and mix well. Rub the fish with the spice mixture and place in a shallow dish. Marinate, covered, for several hours. Place the fish on a grill rack. Grill until the fish flakes easily and is lightly seared on the bottom. Place each fish fillet on one-half of each tortilla. Top with lettuce, cabbage and onion. Fold the remaining half of each tortilla over the top and serve with the fruit salsa.

Serves 4

The weak can never forgive. Forgiveness is the attribute of the strong.
—MOHANDAS K. GANDHI

Veal Grillades with Smoked Gouda Grits

Veal

1¹/2 pounds veal steak
All-purpose flour for dredging
Creole seasoning to taste
2 tablespoons olive oil
¹/3 cup finely chopped celery
¹/3 cup finely chopped green
 bell pepper
¹/3 cup finely chopped yellow onion
1 (8-ounce) can tomato sauce
¹/4 teaspoon thyme
1 bay leaf

Smoked Gouda Grits

3¹/2 cups water
Salt to taste
1 cup quick-cooking grits
1 cup (4 ounces) shredded smoked
 Gouda cheese
2 to 4 tablespoons salted
 butter, softened
Pepper to taste
Louisiana hot pepper sauce to taste

To prepare the grillades, cut the veal into 3×3-inch cutlets. Dredge in a mixture of the flour and Creole seasoning. Fry in the olive oil in a skillet until golden brown. Remove the veal to a plate, reserving the drippings in the skillet. Sauté the celery, bell pepper and onion in the reserved drippings until the onion is translucent. Add the tomato sauce, thyme and bay leaf. Return the veal to the skillet and coat with the sauce. Add enough water to cover. Simmer for 30 to 40 minutes or until the veal is tender and the gravy is thickened. Remove and discard the bay leaf.

To prepare the grits, bring the water and salt to a boil in a medium saucepan. Add the grits gradually, stirring constantly. Reduce the heat to medium-low. Cook, covered, for 5 to 7 minutes or until thickened, stirring occasionally. Add the cheese and butter. Cook until melted, stirring constantly. Remove from the heat. Season with salt and pepper. Cover until serving time.

To serve, spoon the grits onto serving plates. Add the grillades and douse with hot pepper sauce. (Note: If you are not a grits lover, serve the grillades over creamy mashed potatoes.)

Serves 4 to 6

*Never throw mud. Even if you miss your mark,
you will still have dirty hands.*

—ANONYMOUS

Herb-Crusted Beef Tenderloin with Red Wine Mushroom Sauce

Beef

1 (3 1/2-pound) beef tenderloin,
  at room temperature
1 tablespoon extra-virgin olive oil
2 cups salt
3 tablespoons fresh rosemary,
  coarsely chopped
3 tablespoons dried pink
  peppercorns, crushed
1 1/2 cups all-purpose flour
2 egg whites
1/2 cup plus 2 tablespoons water

Red Wine Mushroom Sauce

2 ounces dried mushrooms
1 1/2 cups boiling water
1/3 cup sugar
1/3 cup red wine vinegar
1 cup dry red wine
1 tablespoon unsalted butter, softened
1 tablespoon all-purpose flour
1 cup beef broth
1/4 cup heavy cream
1 large shallot, finely chopped
1 tablespoon unsalted butter
Salt and pepper to taste

To prepare the beef, rinse the beef and pat dry. Heat the olive oil in a large skillet over medium-high heat until hot but not smoking. Add the beef and cook for 8 minutes or until brown on all sides, turning frequently. Remove to a shallow baking pan brushed with olive oil. Let stand for 10 minutes. Whisk the salt, rosemary, peppercorns and flour in a bowl. Add the egg whites and water and mix until the consistency of paste. Pat onto the top and sides of the beef to coat completely. Bake at 450 degrees on a rack in the upper third of the oven for 30 minutes or to 125 degrees on a meat thermometer for medium-rare. Remove from the oven and let stand for 5 minutes.

To prepare the sauce, mix the mushrooms and boiling water in a small heatproof bowl. Let stand for 20 minutes or until softened. Remove with a slotted spoon to a plate and set aside. Pour the mushroom liquid into a cup, leaving any sediment or solids in the bottom of the bowl and set aside. Cook the sugar in a medium saucepan over medium heat for 1 minute or until melted and pale yellow, stirring constantly. Continue to cook for 2 minutes or until the sugar turns amber caramel in color; do not stir. Carefully pour the vinegar down the side of the pan. The caramel will seize. Simmer until the caramel melts. Add the wine and reserved mushroom liquid. Cook for 15 minutes or until reduced to 2/3 cup. Stir in a mixture of 1 tablespoon butter and the flour. Add the broth and cream. Simmer for 5 minutes or until the sauce is reduced to 1 1/2 cups, whisking constantly. Remove from the heat and keep warm. Sauté the shallot and reserved mushrooms in 1 tablespoon butter in a large skillet over medium-high heat for 4 minutes or until golden brown. Reserve 1/4 of the mushrooms in a bowl. Add the sauce to the remaining mushrooms. Cook over medium-high heat for 3 minutes, scraping the brown bits from the bottom of the pan. Season with salt and pepper. Remove the crust from the beef. Slice the beef 1/4 inch thick and arrange on a serving platter. Spoon some of the sauce over the beef and top with the reserved mushrooms. Serve with the remaining sauce.

Serves 8

While we try to teach our children all about life, our children teach us what life is all about.

—ANGELA SCHWINDT

Balsamic Steaks with Cheese Sauce

2/3 cup balsamic vinaigrette
1/4 cup fig preserves
4 (6- to 8-ounce) boneless beef
* rib-eye steaks*

1 teaspoon salt
1 teaspoon freshly ground pepper
1 (6-ounce) container buttery garlic-
* and-herb spreadable cheese*

Process the vinaigrette and preserves in a blender until smooth. Pour over the steaks in a shallow dish or large sealable plastic bag. Cover or seal and marinate in the refrigerator for 2 hours or longer. Drain the steaks, discarding the marinade. Place the steaks on a grill rack. Grill, covered with the grill lid, over medium-high heat for 5 to 7 minutes on each side or to the desired degree of doneness. Remove to a serving platter. Sprinkle with the salt and pepper and keep warm. Heat the cheese in a small saucepan over low heat for 2 to 4 minutes or until melted, stirring frequently. Serve with the steaks.

Serves 4

There are only two lasting bequests we can hope to give our children. One is roots; the other, wings.

—HODDING CARTER

Royal Rack of Lamb with 3 herbs

2 tablespoons Creole mustard
2 tablespoons local honey
Juice of 1 lemon
1/8 teaspoon finely chopped fresh thyme
1/8 teaspoon finely chopped fresh oregano
1/8 teaspoon finely chopped fresh rosemary
Salt and freshly cracked pepper to taste
1 (3- to 4-pound) rack of lamb
12 shallots
12 garlic cloves
1 tablespoon extra-virgin olive oil

Whisk the mustard, honey and lemon juice in a bowl until blended. Mix the thyme, oregano, rosemary, salt and pepper together. Pierce the lamb all over with the tip of a small knife or sharp fork. Rub with a generous amount of the herb mixture. Spoon the mustard mixture over the lamb. Place in a pan. Chill, covered, for several hours.

Place the lamb meat side up on a rack in a roasting pan. Surround with the shallots and garlic and drizzle with the olive oil. Roast at 400 degrees for 45 to 60 minutes or to 145 degrees on a meat thermometer for medium-rare or to 160 degrees for medium, basting every 10 minutes. (It would be a sin to cook lamb past the stage of medium. But then there is always confession.) Remove from the oven and let stand for 5 minutes before serving. Carve the lamb into two chops per person. Spoon the shallots and garlic over each plate.

Serves 4

Children learn to smile from their parents.
—SHINICHI SUZUKI

Grilled Pork Tenderloin with Creole Mustard, Rosemary and Apple Marinade

1/4 cup frozen apple juice concentrate
2 tablespoons Creole mustard
1 tablespoon extra-virgin olive oil
2 tablespoons fresh rosemary, chopped
4 garlic cloves, minced
Creole seasoning to taste
2 pounds pork tenderloins, fat trimmed
1 tablespoon minced shallot
3 tablespoons port
2 tablespoons balsamic vinegar
1 1/2 teaspoons Creole mustard
1 tablespoon extra-virgin olive oil
Salt and freshly ground pepper to taste

Whisk the apple juice concentrate, 2 tablespoons mustard, 1 tablespoon olive oil, the rosemary, garlic and Creole seasoning in a small bowl. Reserve 3 tablespoons of the marinade for basting. Place the pork in a shallow glass dish. Add the remaining marinade, turning to coat. Marinate, covered, in the refrigerator for 30 minutes or up to 2 hours, turning several times. Drain the pork, discarding the marinade. Place the pork on a grill or broiler rack. Grill or broil for 20 minutes or until cooked through, turning several times and basting with the 3 tablespoons reserved marinade. Place on a platter and let stand for 5 minutes before carving into slices.

Whisk the shallot, port, vinegar, 1 1/2 teaspoons mustard, 1 tablespoon olive oil, Creole seasoning, salt and pepper in a small bowl until blended. Drizzle over the pork to serve.

Serves 6

Children are our most valuable natural resource.

—HERBERT HOOVER

Palace Pork Chops with Cajun Cranberry Chutney

Cajun Cranberry Chutney
1/4 cup dried peaches, finely chopped
1/2 cup packed brown sugar
1 cup water
3 cups fresh cranberries
1 green apple, peeled and chopped
1 teaspoon lemon zest
1/4 cup fresh lemon juice
1/2 teaspoon ginger
1/2 teaspoon red pepper flakes, crushed

Pork
1/4 cup soy sauce
1/4 cup bourbon
2 tablespoons brown sugar
2 garlic cloves, cut into quarters
6 to 8 center-cut pork chops,
    cut 1 inch thick

To prepare the chutney, combine the dried peaches, brown sugar and water in a saucepan. Bring to a boil and reduce the heat. Simmer for 5 minutes, stirring constantly. Stir in the cranberries, apple and lemon zest. Cook for 10 to 15 miinutes or until tender. Add the lemon juice, ginger and red pepper flakes. Spoon into a glass serving bowl. Chill, covered with plastic wrap, until serving time.

To prepare the pork, mix the soy sauce, bourbon, 2 tablespoons brown sugar and the garlic in a bowl. Pour over the pork chops in a shallow dish. Marinate, covered, in the refrigerator for 1 hour or longer, turning occasionally. Drain the pork, discarding the marinade. Place the pork on a grill rack. Grill for 5 minutes on each side or until cooked through. Serve with the chutney. (Note: This dish is great served with a holiday corn bread dressing. The chutney may also be served at room temperature.)

Serves 6 to 8

You learn many things from children.
How much patience you have, for instance.

—FRANKLIN P. JONES

Stuffed Whole Cabbage

2 small heads cabbage (about 2 pounds each)
12 ounces ground beef
4 ounces ground pork
1 cup stewed tomatoes
1/2 cup cooked rice
2 tablespoons minced onion
1 tablespoon vinegar
1 tablespoon sugar
1 tablespoon salt
1/4 teaspoon freshly cracked pepper
1/2 cup water

Trim off the outside leaves of the cabbage, reserving two large leaves for topping. Cut a wedge from each at the stem end and remove the core, forming a large cavity. Mix the ground beef, ground pork, tomatoes, rice, onion, vinegar, sugar, salt and pepper in a bowl. Fill each cabbage with the ground beef mixture. Place a reserved cabbage leaf over the top of each. Place in a baking dish and add the water. Bake, covered, at 350 degrees for 1 1/2 to 2 hours or until the cabbage is tender and the filling is cooked through.

Serves 6

When love and skill work together, expect a masterpiece.

—JOHN RUSKIN

Ryan Street Red Beans and Rice

2 pounds dried red kidney beans
4 to 5 quarts water
4 garlic cloves, finely chopped
2 onions, finely chopped
1 bay leaf
Creole seasoning to taste

1/4 cup packed brown sugar
1 (10-ounce) can tomatoes with
   green chiles
2 pounds smoked sausage, sliced
10 cups cooked rice
Louisiana hot pepper sauce to taste

Sort and rinse the beans. Place the beans in a 7-quart Dutch oven. Add the water, garlic, onions, bay leaf and Creole seasoning. Simmer for 2 hours or until the beans are soft, adding additional water as needed. Add the brown sugar, tomatoes with green chiles and sausage. Simmer for 1 hour, skimming the surface as needed and mashing a small portion of the beans after 40 minutes to thicken the gravy, if desired. Remove and discard the bay leaf. Serve over the rice with hot pepper sauce.

Serves 10

The only thing worth stealing is a kiss from a sleeping child.

—JOE HOULDSWORTH

Cranberry-Barbecued Chicken

3 pounds chicken breasts, skin
   removed
1/2 teaspoon salt
1/2 teaspoon pepper

2 ribs celery, chopped
1 cup barbecue sauce
1 yellow onion, chopped
2 cups whole cranberry sauce

Place the chicken in a 3- to 6-quart slow cooker. Sprinkle with salt and pepper. Add the celery, barbecue sauce, onion and cranberry sauce. Cook, covered, on Low for 6 to 8 hours or until the chicken is cooked through.

Serves 4

Big shots are only little shots who kept on shooting.

—CHRISTOPHER MORLEY

Sweet and Jazzy Chicken

6 slices bacon
8 boneless chicken breasts
All-purpose flour for dredging
1/3 cup honey
3 tablespoons Creole mustard
1 teaspoon curry powder
Salt and cayenne pepper or black pepper to taste
Shredded cheese of choice

Cook the bacon in a skillet over medium heat for 8 minutes or until crisp. Remove the bacon to paper towels to drain, reserving the drippings in the skillet. Dredge the chicken in the flour, shaking off the excess. Cook in the reserved drippings over low heat for 10 minutes or until brown on all sides. Place the chicken in an 8×8×2-inch baking dish. Bake at 350 degrees for 30 minutes.

Combine the honey, mustard, curry powder, salt and cayenne pepper in a small bowl and mix well. Coat the chicken with the honey mixture. Bake for 15 minutes or until the chicken is cooked through. Remove from the oven and top with cheese. Crumble the bacon over the top. Let stand, covered, for 10 to 15 minutes before serving to seal in the juices.

Serves 4 to 6

Reflect upon your blessings, of which you have plenty, not on your past misfortunes, of which everyone has some.
—CHARLES DICKENS

Chicken de la Vigne
(Chicken from the Vineyard)

2 tablespoons unsalted butter
1 tablespoon olive oil
6 boneless skinless chicken breasts
1/3 cup white zinfandel or blush wine
3/4 cup heavy cream
1/4 cup mascarpone cheese or cream cheese
1 teaspoon dried thyme, finely crumbled, or
      1 tablespoon fresh whole thyme leaves
Salt and freshly ground pepper to taste
8 ounces seedless red grapes, cut into halves
Chopped fresh parsley to taste

Heat the butter and olive oil in a sauté pan over medium-high heat. Add the
chicken. Sauté for 5 minutes or until light brown on all sides. Add the wine. Bring to a
boil, stirring constantly to prevent burning. Stir in the cream, cheese, thyme, salt and
pepper. Reduce the heat. Simmer, covered, for 5 minutes or until the sauce thickens
slightly. Stir in the grapes. Simmer for 5 minutes or until the grapes are heated through
and the chicken is cooked through but still moist and tender. Sprinkle with parsley.

Serves 4 to 6

Level with your child by being honest.
Nobody spots a phony quicker than a child.

—MARY MACCRACKEN

"Can't Be Beat" Chicken-Fried Chicken

1 pound chicken breast
   cutlets, tenderized
1 cup buttermilk
1 1/2 tablespoon mixture of finely
   chopped parsley, tarragon
   and thyme
1/4 cup yellow cornmeal
1/4 cup all-purpose flour

1/2 teaspoon salt
1 teaspoon pepper
1/4 cup vegetable oil
2 teaspoons all-purpose flour
3/4 cup chicken broth
1/2 cup buttermilk
Salt and pepper to taste

Place the chicken in a shallow dish. Add 1 cup buttermilk and the herbs. Soak, covered, in the refrigerator for 1 to 2 hours to tenderize. Mix the cornmeal, 1/4 cup flour, 1/2 teaspoon salt and 1 teaspoon pepper in a shallow dish. Drain the chicken, discarding the buttermilk. Dredge the chicken in the flour mixture, patting the coating onto the chicken with your hands. Heat 2 tablespoons of the oil in a large skillet over medium-high heat. Add half the chicken. Cook for 6 minutes or until cooked through, turning once. Remove to a platter and keep warm. Repeat with the remaining 2 tablespoons oil and the remaining chicken.

Stir 2 teaspoons flour into the pan drippings. Cook for 1 minute, stirring constantly. Whisk in the broth and 1/2 cup buttermilk. Simmer for 2 minutes, stirring to scrape up the brown bits from the bottom of the skillet. Sprinkle with salt and pepper to taste. Serve over the chicken.

Serves 4

Ability is what you're capable of doing. Motivation determines what you do. Attitude tells how well you will do it.

—LOU HOLTZ

French Fricassee
(A Rustic Country Dish)

Bouquet Garni

8 leek leaves, white portions removed
12 sprigs of thyme
12 sprigs of parsley
4 bay leaves

Fricassee

1 (4-pound) roasting hen or chicken
Kosher salt or sea salt to taste
3/4 teaspoon pepper
1 tablespoon unsalted butter
1 slice bacon, cut into 1-inch pieces
1/2 cup apple brandy
2 cups chicken broth
1 (750-milliliter) bottle red wine (pinot noir or burgundy)
2 garlic cloves, cut into halves
24 ounces fresh mushrooms, stems removed
2 cups chicken broth
Pepper to taste
2 tablespoons unsalted butter
3 tablespoons all-purpose flour

To prepare the bouquet garni, flatten the leek leaves. Place three thyme sprigs, three parsley sprigs and one bay leaf in each of four leek leaves. Top each with one of the remaining leek leaves and tie at 2-inch intervals with string. (If time is an issue, dried herbs may be used.)

To prepare the fricassee, trim any excess fat from the hen. Remove and mince the giblets; set aside. Discard the neck. Remove the skin from the hen. Cut the hen into quarters. Sprinkle with kosher salt and 3/4 teaspoon pepper (keeping in mind that the chicken broth has an abundance of salt already). Heat 1 tablespoon butter in a large Dutch oven over medium heat. Add the hen. Cook for 10 minutes or until brown on all sides. Remove the hen to a platter.

Add the bacon to the drippings in the Dutch oven. Cook until the bacon is crisp. Return the hen to the Dutch oven. Add the bouquet garni, reserved giblets, brandy, 2 cups broth, the wine and garlic. Bring to a boil and reduce the heat. Simmer, covered, for 1 1/2 hours. Remove the hen from the wine mixture and chill, covered, in the refrigerator. Cover and chill the wine mixture for 8 to 24 hours.

Discard the bouquet garni from the wine mixture. Skim the solidified fat from the surface and discard. Combine the mushrooms and 2 cups broth in a large nonstick skillet. Bring to a boil and reduce the heat. Simmer, partially covered, for 30 minutes. Cook, uncovered, for 10 minutes or until the liquid almost evaporates. Sprinkle with kosher salt and pepper to taste. Bring the wine mixture to a boil and reduce the heat. Simmer for 20 minutes. Mix 2 tablespoons butter and the flour in a small bowl to form a paste. Whisk in 1/4 cup of the wine mixture until blended. Add the butter mixture to the remaining wine mixture. Bring to a boil and reduce the heat. Simmer for 10 minutes. Add the hen and mushrooms. Bring to a boil and reduce the heat. Simmer for 10 minutes or until heated through. (*Note: French Fricassee, coq au vin—the quintessential French comfort food—is traditionally made with red wine and older roosters. However, a hen or chicken can be used as well. For a little variation, try using Champagne instead of the red wine for Coq au Champagne.*)

Serves 4

If you fell down yesterday, stand up today.

—H. G. WELLS

Cheesy Chicken with Spinach

1 (10-ounce) package frozen chopped spinach, thawed
1/2 cup (2 ounces) shredded smoked Gouda or
    Swiss cheese
1/4 teaspoon nutmeg
4 chicken breasts (2 1/2 to 3 pounds total)
1/2 teaspoon salt
1/4 teaspoon pepper
2 teaspoons butter, melted

Drain the spinach in a strainer. Squeeze out the excess moisture using paper towels or a clean kitchen towel until the spinach is dry. Combine the spinach, cheese and nutmeg in a medium bowl and mix well. Loosen the skin from the chicken by inserting your fingers between the skin and flesh. Gently separate in the center, leaving the skin attached at the ends. Spread one-fourth of the spinach mixture evenly between the skin and flesh of each breast using your fingers. Smooth the skin over the breasts, tucking under the loose areas. Place skin side up in a 9×9-inch baking pan sprayed with nonstick cooking spray. Sprinkle with the salt and pepper. Drizzle with the butter. Bake at 375 degrees for 45 to 55 minutes or until the juice from the chicken runs clear. *(Note: You can also make this recipe using boneless skinless chicken breasts. Cut a horizontal slit through the thickest portion of each breast to form a pocket. Spoon about 2 tablespoons of the spinach mixture into each pocket and bake as directed above.)*

Serves 4

*Parents can only give good advice or put them
on the right paths, but the final
forming of a person's character lies in their own hands.*

—ANNE FRANK

"Nu-awlins" Chicken and Dumplings

5 pounds chicken (bone-in legs,
 breasts and thighs)
4 cups chicken broth or stock
1 cup chopped onion
1 cup chopped celery
Salt and pepper to taste

3 cups milk
1 cup heavy cream
5 cups all-purpose flour
Pinch of salt
1/2 cup shortening, chilled
6 tablespoons cold water

Bring the chicken, broth, onion, celery, salt and pepper to taste to a boil in a large stockpot over high heat, skimming off the top. Reduce the heat. Simmer, covered, for 2 to 3 hours or until the chicken is very tender. Remove from the heat to cool.

Remove the chicken from the stock. Chop the chicken, discarding the skin and bones; set aside. Strain the stock, discarding the solids. Return the strained stock to the stockpot. Add the milk and cream. Bring almost to a boil over medium heat. Reduce the heat to low and simmer.

Mix the flour and pinch of salt in a large bowl. Cut in the shortening with a pastry blender or fork until the mixture resembles coarse cornmeal. Add just enough water to make the dough the consistency of pie dough. Roll the dough into a rectangle 1/8 inch thick on a lightly floured surface. Cut into strips 4 inches long and 1 1/2 inches wide.

Bring the stock mixture to a boil. Drop in the dumplings a few at a time until all have been added. Add the chopped chicken. Reduce the heat to low. Simmer for 35 to 45 minutes or until the dumplings are tender, gently stirring only when necessary to keep the dumplings submerged and to prevent sticking.

Serves 6

Follow your bliss. Find where it is and
don't be afraid to follow it.

—JOSEPH CAMPBELL

Prien Chicken Potpie

1/3 cup unsalted butter
1/3 cup all-purpose flour
4 cups chicken stock
Salt and pepper to taste
3 small Yukon Gold potatoes, peeled
    and cut into 1/2-inch-thick pieces
2 carrots, cut into 1/2-inch-thick pieces
3 1/2 cups chopped cooked chicken
    (1/2-inch-thick pieces)

1 cup frozen small green peas
1 cup fresh or frozen whole
    kernel corn
1/4 cup finely chopped
    flat-leaf parsley
1 (14-ounce) package frozen
    puff pastry
1 egg
1 teaspoon salt

Melt the butter in a large saucepan over medium-high heat. Whisk in the flour for 2 minutes or until blended. Add the stock. Increase the heat to high and bring to a boil. Cook until thickened and smooth, whisking constantly. Season with salt and pepper to taste. Remove from the heat. Cover and set aside.

Place the potatoes and carrots in separate saucepans and add water to cover each. Sprinkle with salt to taste. Bring to a boil. Cook for 5 minutes or until almost tender. Drain and rinse separately under cold running water. Add the potatoes, carrots, chicken, peas, corn, parsley, salt and pepper to taste to the sauce and mix well. Divide the mixture evenly among four 2-cup ramekins.

Roll the puff pastry into a circle 1/8 inch thick. Cut into four circles 1/2 inch larger in diameter than the rim of each ramekin. Lightly beat the egg and 1 teaspoon salt in a small bowl. Lightly brush one side of each circle with the egg mixture. Place one circle brushed side down on each ramekin and press firmly against the outside to seal. Cut a small "X" in the center to allow steam to escape. Brush the tops with the remaining egg mixture.

Place the ramekins on a rimmed baking sheet lined with foil. Bake on the middle oven rack at 400 degrees for 45 minutes or until the pastry is golden brown. Place each ramekin on a serving plate and serve immediately.

Serves 4

Making the decision to have a child—it's momentous. It is to decide forever to have your heart go walking outside your body.

—ELIZABETH STONE

Chicken Étouffée

1 tablespoon butter
2 tablespoons vegetable oil
2 to 3 pounds chicken breasts, cut into 2-inch pieces
1 cup chopped onion
1/2 cup chopped celery
1/2 cup chopped bell pepper
2 tablespoons chopped garlic
3/4 cup roux
4 cups chicken broth (1 quart)
10 ounces beer
2 teaspoons brown sugar
1/4 cup Creole hot sauce
1 tablespoon Worcestershire sauce
1/4 cup parsley, chopped
Salt and black or red pepper to taste
4 cups cooked rice

Melt the butter in the oil in a large stockpot. Add the chicken, onion, celery, bell pepper and garlic. Sauté over medium-high heat for 15 to 20 minutes or until the vegetables are tender. Add the roux and 1 cup of the broth. Cook over medium heat for 10 minutes. Stir in the remaining broth, beer, brown sugar, hot sauce, Worcestershire sauce, parsley, salt and pepper. Cook over medium-low heat for 40 minutes. Reduce the heat and simmer for 20 minutes longer. Serve over the rice. (Note: If the gravy is not thick enough, add a mixture of 2 tablespoons cornstarch dissolved in a small amount of water and return to a boil. Turn off the heat and stir.)

Serves 4

When you develop yourself to the point where your belief in yourself is so strong that you know you can accomplish anything you put yourself into, your future will be unlimited.

—BRIAN TRACY

Wine Country Cornish Hens

1¹/2 pounds mixed red and green seedless grapes
8 shallots, peeled and cut into halves, or
    3 to 4 small onions, peeled and cut into quarters
6 sprigs of thyme
2 tablespoons extra-virgin olive oil
Salt and freshly cracked pepper to taste
4 (1- to 1¹/4-pound) Cornish game hens
Thyme leaves to taste

Spread the grapes, shallots, thyme sprigs, olive oil, salt and pepper on a baking
sheet. Tie the hen legs with kitchen twine and place breast side up on the grape mixture.
Season generously with salt and pepper. Sprinkle with thyme leaves. Roast at 450 degrees
for 30 to 35 minutes or until a meat thermometer inserted into the thickest part of the
leg registers 160 degrees, basting occasionally with the pan juices.

Serves 4

One generation plants the trees; another gets the shade.

—CHINESE PROVERB

Lafitte's Rice Dressing

3 sets chicken giblets, ground, or
    1^1/2 cups ground beef, veal or pork
2 large onions, ground
1 cup ground celery
6 tablespoons butter
^{1}/4 cup oyster liquid
2 oysters, ground, or
    1 small eggplant, peeled, chopped and boiled
^{1}/2 cup parsley, finely chopped
2 garlic cloves, finely chopped
^{1}/2 cup ground green onions
Creole seasoning to taste
Louisiana hot pepper sauce
4 cups cooked rice

Sauté the giblets, onions and celery in the butter in a skillet until the giblets are brown and the vegetables are soft. Stir in the oyster liquid, oysters, parsley, garlic and ground green onions. Simmer, covered, for 10 minutes. Stir in the Creole seasoning, hot pepper sauce and rice. Cook until heated through. Spoon into a greased baking dish. Bake at 350 degrees for 20 minutes. Garnish with finely chopped green onions.

Serves 8

If our American way of life fails the child, it fails us all.

—PEARL S. BUCK

Duck Stroganoff

2 ducks, cut up
1 tablespoon all-purpose flour
1$^1/_2$ teaspoons salt
$^1/_2$ teaspoon pepper
3 tablespoons olive oil
3 tablespoons butter
1 white onion, chopped
$^1/_2$ teaspoon thyme
$^1/_2$ teaspoon sweet basil
$^1/_2$ teaspoon parsley flakes
1 cup sauterne (French dessert wine)
1 cup whipping cream
Hot cooked fettuccini

Coat the ducks with a mixture of the flour, salt and pepper. Brown in the olive oil and butter in a Dutch oven. Add the onion, thyme, basil and parsley. Heat the wine in a saucepan and pour over the ducks. Bake, covered, at 350 degrees for 1 hour. Stir in the cream. Bake for 20 to 25 minutes or until the mixture appears curdled. Serve over fettuccini.

Serves 6

The bond that links your true family is not one of blood, but of respect and joy in each other's life.

—RICHARD BACH

Sides

Cooking Up Fun With Kids

SALT PAINT

2 teaspoons salt
1 teaspoon liquid starch
Few drops of tempera paint

Combine the salt, liquid starch and tempera paint in a bowl and
mix well. Apply the mixture with a brush to the object to be painted.
Let stand until dry.

Asparagus Gratin

2 pounds large asparagus
3 tablespoons olive oil
1 tablespoon fresh lemon juice
Salt and pepper to taste
1 tablespoon butter
1 garlic clove, minced
1 tablespoon minced shallot
1 tablespoon heavy cream
3/4 cup (3 ounces) freshly grated Parmigiano-Reggiano cheese or
   Parmesan cheese
2 tablespoons coarsely shaved Parmigiano-Reggiano cheese or
   Parmesan cheese
2 tablespoons unseasoned dry bread crumbs

Cut off the tough ends of the asparagus and peel the lower half. Toss the asparagus with the olive oil, lemon juice, salt and pepper in a bowl until coated. Place in a baking dish. Roast at 450 degrees in the top one-third of the oven for 12 minutes or until light brown and tender-crisp. Remove from the oven and drain off the excess oil. Maintain the oven temperature.

Melt the butter in a 2-quart saucepan over medium heat. Add the garlic and shallot and sauté for 2 minutes. Add the cream. Simmer for 6 minutes or until the mixture is reduced by one-third. Stir in 3/4 cup Parmigiano-Reggiano cheese, salt and pepper.

Arrange the asparagus spears in an ovenproof serving dish. Spoon the sauce over the asparagus, leaving the tips and bases uncovered. Sprinkle with 2 tablespoons Parmigiano-Reggiano cheese and the bread crumbs. Bake for 5 minutes or until golden brown. Serve hot.

Serves 6

Character is the real foundation of all worthwhile success.

—JOHN HAYS HAMMOND

Zesty Farm Fresh Green Bean Casserole

1 1/2 tablespoons unsalted butter
3 tablespoons all-purpose flour
1 1/2 cups milk
3 to 4 teaspoons ranch salad dressing mix
Salt and white pepper to taste
1 cup finely chopped onion
2 garlic cloves, finely chopped
1 1/2 cups sliced fresh mushrooms
1 1/4 pounds fresh green beans, cooked
1 cup fresh bread crumbs, toasted

Melt the butter in a small saucepan over low heat. Stir in the flour. Cook for 1 to 2 minutes, whisking constantly. Stir in the milk. Bring to a boil. Cook for 1 to 2 minutes or until thickened, whisking constantly. Stir in the salad dressing mix, salt and white pepper. Remove from the heat and set aside.

Sauté the onion and garlic in a medium skillet sprayed with nonstick cooking spray over medium-high heat for 2 to 3 minutes or until tender. Remove one-half of the onion mixture to a bowl and reserve. Add the mushrooms to the remaining onion mixture in the skillet. Cook for 5 minutes or until the mushrooms are tender.

Layer the mushroom mixture, green beans and white sauce in a 1 1/2-quart baking dish. Toss the bread crumbs with the reserved onion mixture and sprinkle over the top. Bake at 350 degrees for 20 to 30 minutes or until heated through.

Serves 6

There are no shortcuts to any place worth going.

—BEVERLY SILLS

Best-Ever Broccoli au Gratin with Crab

12 slices bread
2 1/2 cups milk
1 cup mayonnaise
7 hard-cooked eggs, finely chopped
1 pound fresh lump crab meat,
   shells removed and crab meat flaked
1/4 cup finely chopped onion
1 tablespoon plus 1 teaspoon chopped fresh parsley
2 1/2 cups fresh broccoli florets, cooked and drained
1 cup (4 ounces) shredded sharp Cheddar cheese

Trim the crusts from the bread. Cut the bread into 1/2-inch cubes. Combine the bread cubes, milk and mayonnaise in a bowl and mix well. Chill, covered, for 30 minutes. Stir in the eggs, crab meat, onion and parsley. Arrange the broccoli in a lightly greased 9×13-inch baking dish. Spoon the crab meat mixture over the broccoli. Bake at 325 degrees for 40 minutes. Sprinkle with the cheese and bake for 5 minutes longer or until the cheese melts. (*Note: You may use two 10-ounce packages frozen broccoli.*)

Serves 5

If you have one eye on yesterday and one eye on tomorrow,
you're going to be cockeyed today.

—Anonymous

Shaved Blackened Brussels Sprouts

2 slices bacon
Salt and pepper to taste
24 small brussels sprouts, trimmed
    and quartered

2 tablespoons (or more) extra-virgin
    olive oil
1/4 cup (1 ounce) shredded cheese
    of choice

Cook the bacon sprinkled with salt and pepper in a large skillet over medium-high heat until crisp. Remove the bacon, reserving the drippings in the skillet. Crumble the bacon. Coat the brussels sprouts with the olive oil and sprinkle with salt and pepper. Add to the reserved drippings. Cook over medium-high heat for 5 to 10 minutes or until light brown and caramelized slightly, stirring constantly. Sprinkle with the cheese and bacon.

Serves 4

*If you can read the handwriting on the wall, your children are
old enough to know better.*

—ANONYMOUS

Carrots Cointreau

30 fresh baby carrots, peeled
Salt to taste
2 tablespoons Cointreau
1/4 cup brandy

1/4 cup honey
1 1/2 tablespoons fresh lemon juice
2 tablespoons fresh parsley, chopped

Parboil the carrots in boiling salted water in a saucepan for 5 minutes; drain. Place in a buttered 1 1/2-quart baking dish. Combine the Cointreau, brandy, honey and lemon juice in a small bowl and mix well. Pour over the carrots and toss to coat. Bake at 350 degrees for 15 minutes. Stir and sprinkle with the parsley.

Serves 6

*Anyone who stops learning is old, whether at twenty or eighty.
Anyone who keeps learning stays young.*

—HENRY FORD

Cauliflower with Gruyère Cheese and Toasted Almonds

White Sauce
1/4 cup (1/2 stick) unsalted butter
1/4 cup all-purpose flour
2 cups milk, scalded
1 small onion (optional)
2 or 3 cloves (optional)
1 small bay leaf
1/16 teaspoon crumbled thyme leaves
Salt and white pepper to taste
Nutmeg to taste

Cauliflower
1 head cauliflower
Salt to taste
Dash of cayenne pepper
3/4 cup (3 ounces) shredded
   Gruyère cheese
1/2 cup sliced almonds, toasted

To prepare the sauce, melt the butter in a medium saucepan over low heat. Heat until the butter begins to foam. Add the flour all at once and mix well with a wooden spoon. Cook over low heat for 3 to 4 minutes, stirring constantly. Remove from the heat. Let stand for 15 minutes. Return to medium-low heat. Add the scalded milk all at once and simmer, stirring gently with a whisk or wooden spoon. Pierce the onion with the cloves. Add the onion, bay leaf and thyme to the milk mixture. Cook over low heat for 15 to 20 minutes or until smooth and thickened, stirring constantly. Strain the sauce through a fine mesh strainer, discarding the solids. Add salt, white pepper and nutmeg. Measure 1 1/2 cups of the white sauce, reserving the remaining sauce to use for another purpose.

To prepare the cauliflower, remove the leaves and woody stem from the cauliflower. Cook, covered, in a small amount of boiling salted water in a saucepan for 20 to 25 minutes or until tender; drain. Place in a baking dish. Stir 1/2 cup of the cheese into the white sauce. Pour over the cauliflower. Sprinkle with the cayenne pepper, remaining 1/4 cup cheese and the almonds. Bake at 350 degrees for 10 minutes.

Serves 6

Try not to become a man of success but a man of value.

—ALBERT EINSTEIN

Cameron Corn "Mok-shoo"

1/2 cup chopped onion
1/2 cup chopped green bell pepper
1 1/2 teaspoons finely chopped
   fresh garlic
1/4 cup (1/2 stick) butter
1/2 teaspoon all-purpose flour

3 tablespoons finely chopped fresh
   basil, or 1 tablespoon dried basil
3 1/2 cups fresh or frozen whole
   kernel corn
1 (10-ounce) can tomatoes with
   green chiles

Sauté the onion, bell pepper and garlic in the butter in a 2-quart saucepan over medium-high heat. Stir in the flour and basil until blended. Add the corn. Simmer over medium heat until the corn begins to stick to the bottom of the pan, stirring constantly to prevent burning. Add the tomatoes with green chiles and mix well.

Serves 8 to 10

A torn jacket is soon mended; but hard words bruise the heart of a child.

—HENRY WADSWORTH LONGFELLOW

Petite Peas with Pecans and Bacon

4 slices bacon, chopped
1/2 onion, chopped
2 (16-ounce) packages frozen baby
   green peas

1/2 cup water
1 teaspoon Creole seasoning
1 cup pecans, toasted and chopped

Cook the bacon in a large skillet over medium heat until crisp. Remove the bacon to paper towels to drain. Drain the skillet, reserving 1 tablespoon of the drippings in the skillet. Add the onion to the hot drippings. Reduce the heat to medium-low. Cook for 15 minutes or until light brown. Add the peas, water and Creole seasoning. Cook for 10 minutes or until the peas are tender, stirring occasionally. Stir in the bacon and pecans.

Serves 8 to 10

If you find yourself all prepared but unable to get into the action, here is some very sound advice. Get inspired, take charge!

—ANONYMOUS

Soufflé of Potatoes with Blueberries

5 pounds potatoes
Salt to taste
2/3 cup butter
1 large onion, finely chopped
2 cups fresh or frozen blueberries
3 eggs, beaten
1 cup milk
Nutmeg to taste
Pepper to taste
1 cup fresh bread crumbs
1 cup (4 ounces) shredded Cheddar cheese

Peel the potatoes and cut into chunks. Place in a large stockpot and cover with cold water. Add salt. Bring to a boil and reduce the heat. Simmer for 20 minutes or until the potatoes are tender. Melt 2 tablespoons of the butter in a large skillet over medium heat. Add the onion and blueberries. Cook for 10 minutes or until softened, stirring constantly.

Drain the potatoes and return to the stockpot. Add the remaining butter, eggs and milk and mash until smooth. Stir in the blueberry mixture, nutmeg, salt and pepper. Spread in a buttered deep 3-quart baking dish. Mix the bread crumbs and cheese in a bowl. Sprinkle over the potato mixture. Bake at 400 degrees for 30 minutes or until heated through and the cheese melts.

Serves 10

A winner never quits, and a quitter never wins.

—Anonymous

Pontchartrain Potatoes

3 cups potatoes, peeled and sliced
1/2 cup sliced onion
2 tablespoons chopped garlic
1/2 cup (2 ounces) grated
    Parmesan cheese

1/2 cup (2 ounces) shredded
    Monterey Jack cheese
Salt and pepper to taste
2 cups cream

Layer the potatoes, onion and garlic in a baking dish, sprinkling the Parmesan cheese and Monterey Jack cheese between each layer. Sprinkle with salt and pepper. Pour the cream over the top. Bake at 350 degrees for 30 to 40 minutes or until cooked through. Remove from the oven and garnish with chopped green onions.

Serves 6

Minds are like parachutes, they function only when open.

—ANONYMOUS

Rustic Roasted Acorn Squash with Maple Syrup

2 acorn squash
Salt and pepper to taste
Freshly grated nutmeg to taste

1/4 cup (1/2 stick) butter
1 1/2 cups maple syrup

Cut the squash into halves lengthwise, cleaning out and discarding the seeds and strings. Cut a thin slice from the bottom of each half so the squash will sit level. Place on a rimmed baking sheet and sprinkle with salt and pepper. Sprinkle evenly with nutmeg. Place 1 tablespoon butter in each half. Fill each half almost to the top with the maple syrup. Bake at 400 degrees for 1 hour or until tender when pierced with a fork. Serve hot.

Serves 4

Put your ear down close to your soul and listen hard.

—ANNE SEXTON

Green T'mater Pie

Pie Pastry

2 cups all-purpose flour

1 teaspoon salt

2/3 cup plus 2 tablespoons cold butter
  or shortening

5 tablespoons (or more) ice water

Pie

8 green tomatoes, sliced

2 tablespoons fresh lemon juice

1 teaspoon grated lemon zest

1/2 teaspoon salt

1/4 teaspoon cinnamon

3/4 cup sugar

1 tablespoon cornstarch

1 tablespoon butter

To prepare the pastry, mix the flour and salt together. Cut in the butter with a pastry blender or butter knives until the mixture is crumbly and resembles large peas. Add the ice water 1 tablespoon at a time, stirring with a fork until the mixture forms a moist ball. Divide the dough into two equal portions. Tear a piece of plastic wrap larger than a 9-inch pie plate and sprinkle with flour. Place one portion of the dough on the prepared wrap and flatten with your hand. Top with another layer of plastic wrap. Roll with a floured rolling pin into a 12-inch circle. Remove the plastic wrap. Repeat with the remaining portion of dough.

To prepare the pie, cook the tomatoes with the lemon juice, lemon zest, salt and cinnamon in a saucepan for 15 minutes, stirring frequently. Mix the sugar and cornstarch together and add to the tomato mixture. Cook until clear, stirring constantly. Add the butter and cool slightly. Place a 9-inch pie plate over one portion of the dough. Slip your hand under the plastic wrap and flip into the pie plate. Remove the plastic wrap and fit the pastry into the pie plate. Add the tomato mixture. Cover with the remaining pastry, fluting the edge and pricking the top. Bake at 425 degrees for 40 to 50 minutes or until golden brown.

Serves 8

Blessed are those who can give without remembering
and take without forgetting.

—Elizabeth Asquith Bibesco

Tomato Bread Pudding

2 pounds red tomatoes, peeled, seeded and chopped
1/4 cup white zinfandel
3 tablespoons fresh basil leaves, chopped
3 tablespoons brown sugar
1 teaspoon Worcestershire sauce
Pinch of cayenne pepper
1 (1-pound) loaf dry bread, cut into 1-inch cubes
1/4 cup (1/2 stick) unsalted butter, melted
1 cup (4 ounces) shredded Monterey Jack cheese

Combine the tomatoes, wine, basil, brown sugar, Worcestershire sauce and cayenne pepper in a small saucepan and mix well. Simmer over medium-low heat for 10 minutes, stirring occasionally. Combine the bread cubes, butter and cheese in a large bowl and toss to mix. Add the tomato mixture and toss to coat. Spread in an even layer in a greased 8×12-inch baking dish. Bake at 400 degrees for 25 to 30 minutes or until brown. Cut into six pieces and serve warm.

Serves 6

Many of the things you can count on, don't count. Many of the things you can't count on, really count.

—ALBERT EINSTEIN

Lou-Zee-Anna Zucchini and Potato Pancakes

3 cups shredded zucchini (about 3)
1 cup shredded peeled potato (about 1 large)
1/2 cup seasoned bread crumbs
3 tablespoons all-purpose flour
1 teaspoon baking soda
Creole seasoning to taste
3 eggs, beaten
1 small onion, finely chopped
2 garlic cloves, finely chopped
4 tablespoons olive oil

Drain the zucchini and potato in a colander, squeezing to remove excess liquid. Pat dry and set aside. Combine the bread crumbs, flour, baking soda and Creole seasoning in a large bowl. Stir in the eggs until blended. Add the onion, garlic and zucchini mixture and toss to coat.

Heat 2 tablespoons of the olive oil in a large nonstick skillet over medium heat. Drop the batter by one-quarter cupfuls into the skillet. Fry until golden brown on both sides, using the remaining olive oil as needed; drain.

Makes 1 dozen

You will live wisely if you are happy in your lot.

—HORACE

The Saints' Summer Vegetable Bake

4 or 5 ears of corn
1 pound small zucchini, thinly sliced
3/4 cup chopped green bell pepper
3 tomatoes, peeled and coarsely chopped
1 onion, chopped
1 garlic clove, chopped
2 tablespoons olive oil
1 teaspoon Italian seasoning
Salt and pepper to taste
1 1/2 cups bread cubes
1/2 cup (2 ounces) shredded mozzarella cheese

Remove the husks and silk from the corn. Cut the kernels from the ears using a sharp knife. Scrape the ears with a knife to release the liquid. Combine the corn, zucchini, bell pepper, tomatoes, onion, garlic, olive oil, Italian seasoning, salt and pepper in a saucepan and mix well. Cook over medium heat for 10 to 12 minutes or until the corn and zucchini are just cooked through. Spoon into a baking dish. Sprinkle with the bread and cheese. Bake at 350 degrees for 20 to 30 minutes or until the cheese melts and the bread is toasted.

Serves 6

A good goal is like a strenuous exercise—it makes you stretch.
—MARY KAY ASH

Vegetable Ratatouille

2 garlic cloves, finely chopped
2 onions, thinly sliced
2 green bell peppers, cut into thin strips
$1/2$ cup olive oil
2 tablespoons butter (optional)
1 pound eggplant, cut into $3/4$-inch strips
2 zucchini, cut into thin slices
3 tomatoes, coarsely chopped
1 tablespoon fresh parsley, finely chopped
1 teaspoon salt
$1/4$ teaspoon freshly cracked pepper

Sauté the garlic, onions and bell peppers in the olive oil and butter in a large skillet for 15 minutes. Add the eggplant, zucchini, tomatoes, parsley, salt and pepper. Cook until the eggplant is tender and only a small amount of liquid remains, stirring gently occasionally.

Serves 8

My success is measured by my willingness to keep trying.

—ANONYMOUS

McNeese Mac and Cheese

2 tablespoons butter
3 tablespoons all-purpose flour
1 cup half-and-half
Sugar to taste
16 ounces elbow macaroni or
    penne pasta, cooked and drained
2 cups (8 ounces) shredded fontina cheese
2 cups (8 ounces) shredded mozzarella cheese
2 cups (8 ounces) shredded Gruyère cheese
4 ounces Gorgonzola cheese, crumbled

Melt the butter in a saucepan. Add the flour and cook until the butter is absorbed. Stir in the half-and-half and sugar. Cook until thickened, stirring constantly. Pour over the hot pasta and toss to coat. Spoon into a baking dish. Layer the fontina cheese, mozzarella cheese, Gruyère cheese and Gorgonzola cheese one-half at a time over the pasta mixture. Bake at 350 degrees for 30 to 45 minutes or until heated through.

Serves 4 to 6

One today is worth two tomorrows.
—BENJAMIN FRANKLIN

Red Wine Marinara with Pasta

1¹/2 teaspoons minced fresh garlic
2 tablespoons olive oil
¹/2 cup dry red or white wine
2 (15-ounce) cans petite
    diced tomatoes
2 tablespoons fresh basil, chopped
1 tablespoon fresh oregano, chopped
1 teaspoon sugar

¹/4 teaspoon pepper
12 ounces pasta
4 ounces mozzarella cheese, shredded
¹/3 cup freshly grated
    Parmesan cheese
Chopped fresh basil to taste
Freshly grated Parmesan cheese
    to taste

Sauté the garlic in the hot olive oil in a skillet over medium heat for 1 minute or until light brown. Stir in the wine, tomatoes, 2 tablespoons basil, the oregano, sugar and pepper carefully. Bring to a boil and reduce the heat to medium-low. Simmer for 20 minutes or until thickened, stirring occasionally.

Cook the pasta using the package directions; drain. Combine the hot pasta, mozzarella cheese and ¹/3 cup Parmesan cheese in a large serving bowl and toss until the cheese begins to melt. Add the tomato sauce and toss to mix. Sprinkle with basil and Parmesan cheese to taste and serve immediately. (*Note: For Red Wine Tomato and Steak Pasta, prepare the sauce as directed, stirring in 2 cups thinly sliced cooked steak before simmering; use penne pasta. For White Wine Tomato and Clam Pasta, prepare the sauce as directed, using dry white wine instead of the red wine and stirring in two 6-ounce cans chopped clams, drained, just before tossing with the pasta mixture. Use a chianti or merlot for red wine and pinot grigio for white wine.*)

Serves 6

To value his own good opinion, a child has to feel that he is a worthwhile person. He has to have confidence in himself as an individual.

—SIDONIE GRUENBERG

Everything-but-the-Kitchen-Sink Corn Bread Dressing

1 cup finely chopped celery (2 ribs)
1 green bell pepper, finely chopped
1 large white onion, finely chopped
1 bunch green onions, finely chopped
1 cup parsley, finely chopped
4 to 6 garlic cloves, finely chopped
Creole seasoning to taste
Olive oil for sautéing
2 tablespoons butter
12 cups crumbled corn bread

8 to 10 hard-cooked eggs, peeled
  and shredded
6 to 8 teaspoons Fresh Poultry
  Seasoning (see Note), or
  2 teaspoons dried poultry
  seasoning
1 1/2 to 2 quarts canned or homemade
  chicken broth (6 to 8 cups)
6 eggs, lightly beaten

Sauté the celery, bell pepper, onion, green onions, parsley, garlic and Creole seasoning in the olive oil and butter in a skillet over medium heat until the vegetables are just tender. Combine the corn bread, hard-cooked eggs and sautéed vegetables in a large bowl and mix well. Stir in the poultry seasoning. Add enough of the chicken broth to make of the consistency of oatmeal, stirring constantly. Adjust the seasonings to taste. Add the lightly beaten eggs and mix well. Pour into a 9×13-inch baking pan sprayed with nonstick cooking spray. Bake, covered, at 350 degrees for 45 minutes. Bake, uncovered, for 15 minutes or until firm and the top is golden brown. (*Note: For Fresh Poultry Seasoning, mix 2 tablespoons finely chopped parsley, 2 tablespoons finely chopped sage, 2 tablespoons finely chopped thyme, 2 tablespoons finely chopped marjoram, 1 tablespoon finely chopped rosemary, 1 tablespoon finely chopped savory, 1 tablespoon pepper and 1/2 teaspoon nutmeg in a bowl.*)

Serves 12

Sometimes the best deals are the ones you don't make.

—BILL VEECK

Desserts

Cooking Up Fun With Kids

EASY DYE

Rubbing alcohol
Food coloring
Pasta shapes, rice and/or seeds
Waxed paper

Pour a small amount of alcohol into individual containers. Tint the alcohol in each container with food coloring to the desired shade.

Drop the pasta, rice and/or seeds to be dyed into the containers. Let stand for 1 minute.

Remove the objects with a spoon to waxed paper to dry. The alcohol will evaporate quickly, leaving the dyed objects ready to use for art.

Maple Crème Brûlée

4 cups (1 quart) heavy cream
1 vanilla bean
1/2 cup granulated sugar
9 egg yolks
1/3 cup maple syrup
Brown sugar for sprinkling

Heat the cream, vanilla bean and granulated sugar in a saucepan over medium heat until the granulated sugar dissolves, stirring constantly. Do not boil. Remove from the heat and discard the vanilla bean. Whisk the egg yolks and maple syrup in a large bowl until blended. Add the cream mixture gradually, stirring constantly. Divide equally among eight ramekins. Place the ramekins side by side in a baking pan. Add enough warm water to the baking pan to come half way up the sides. Bake at 350 degrees for 45 minutes or until the custard is set. Cool in the refrigerator.

To serve, sprinkle the tops of each custard with brown sugar. Broil or torch until the brown sugar caramelizes.

Serves 8

True wisdom lies in gathering the precious things
out of each day as it goes by.

—E. S. BOUTON

Creole Bread Pudding with Marmalade

3 cups dry French bread cubes
$^1/_4$ cup raisins (optional)
2 tablespoons butter, softened
2 egg yolks
6 tablespoons sugar
$1^1/_4$ cups milk
1 teaspoon vanilla extract
2 egg whites, at room temperature
$^1/_4$ teaspoon cream of tartar
$^1/_4$ cup sugar
Orange marmalade or strawberry preserves (optional)

Moisten the bread cubes with water and squeeze to remove the excess. Combine the bread, raisins and butter in a bowl and mix well. Spoon into a greased 1-quart baking dish. Beat the egg yolks and 6 tablespoons sugar in a mixing bowl. Add the milk and vanilla and mix well. Pour over the bread mixture. Bake at 250 degrees for 45 minutes.

Beat the egg whites and cream of tartar in a mixing bowl until soft peaks form. Add $^1/_4$ cup sugar gradually, beating constantly until stiff peaks form. Spread a thin layer of orange marmalade over the bread pudding. Spread the meringue over the top, sealing to the edge. Bake for 15 minutes.

Serves 6

A mother understands what a child does not say.

—Anonymous

"Praw-leen" Pumpkin Cheesecake

3/4 cup graham cracker crumbs
1/2 cup pecans, finely chopped
1/4 cup packed light brown sugar
1/4 cup (1/2 stick) unsalted butter,
    melted and cooled
1 1/2 cups canned solid-pack pumpkin
3 eggs
1/2 cup packed light brown sugar
2 tablespoons heavy cream
1 teaspoon vanilla extract
1 tablespoon bourbon

1/2 cup granulated sugar
1 tablespoon cornstarch
1 1/2 teaspoons cinnamon
1/2 teaspoon nutmeg
1/2 teaspoon ginger
1/2 teaspoon salt
24 ounces cream cheese, softened
2 cups sour cream
2 tablespoons granulated sugar
1 tablespoon bourbon

Invert the bottom of a 9-inch springform pan to create a flat bottom that will make it easier to remove the cheesecake from the pan; lock on the side. Butter the pan. Combine the graham cracker crumbs, 1/2 cup pecans, 1/4 cup brown sugar and 1/4 cup butter in a bowl and mix well. Press evenly over the bottom and 1/2 inch up the side of the prepared pan. Chill for 1 hour.

Whisk the pumpkin, eggs, 1/2 cup brown sugar, the cream, vanilla and 1 tablespoon bourbon in a bowl until blended. Mix 1/2 cup granulated sugar, the cornstarch, cinnamon, nutmeg, ginger and salt in a large mixing bowl. Add the cream cheese and beat at high speed for 3 minutes or until creamy and smooth. Reduce the speed to medium. Add the pumpkin mixture and beat until smooth. Pour into the crust, smoothing the top. Place the springform pan in a shallow baking pan to prevent any leakage. Bake on the middle oven rack at 350 degrees for 50 to 60 minutes or until set. Remove to a wire rack and cool for 5 minutes. Maintain the oven temperature.

Whisk the sour cream, 2 tablespoons granulated sugar and 1 tablespoon bourbon in a bowl. Spread over the top of the cheesecake. Bake for 5 minutes. Remove from the oven to a wire rack and cool for 3 hours or until completely cool. Chill, covered, for 4 hours or longer before serving.

To serve, remove the side of the pan and bring the cheesecake to room temperature. Garnish with pecan halves.

Serves 8

Adult education will continue as long as children have homework to do.

—ANONYMOUS

"Grand" Cobbler with Pears and Blackberries

2 cups all-purpose flour
1/2 teaspoon salt
1 1/2 teaspoons sugar
1 cup (2 sticks) unsalted butter, cut into cubes
1/2 cup ice water
4 cups fresh Louisiana blackberries
1 1/2 large fresh pears, peeled and chopped
2 cups sugar
2 tablespoons all-purpose flour
1/4 cup Grand Marnier
1/2 cup (1 stick) unsalted butter, cut into cubes
French vanilla ice cream

Combine 2 cups flour, the salt and 1 1/2 teaspoons sugar in a mixing bowl. Cut in 1 cup butter until the mixture resembles coarse crumbs. Add the ice water 1 tablespoon at a time, stirring with a fork until the mixture forms a smooth ball. Wrap the dough tightly in plastic wrap and chill for 30 minutes. Unwrap and place on a lightly floured surface. Divide the dough into two equal portions. Roll each portion into a square 1/8 inch thick. Place one square of the pastry in a 9×9-inch baking pan.

Toss the blackberries and pears with 2 cups sugar, 2 tablespoons flour and the Grand Marnier in a mixing bowl. Spoon into the prepared pan. Dot with 1/2 cup butter. Top with the remaining square of pastry, tucking the edges down into the pan. Bake at 350 degrees for 35 minutes or until the pastry is golden brown. Remove from the oven to cool. Serve with ice cream and garnish with sprigs of fresh mint.

Serves 10

Those who won't be advised, can't be helped.

—ANONYMOUS

Lake Charles Latte Chocolate Custard Cups

Sweetened Whipped Cream
2 cups heavy whipping cream (1 pint)
1/4 cup confectioners' sugar
1/2 teaspoon vanilla extract

Chocolate Custard Cups
6 ounces bittersweet chocolate, chopped
1 1/2 cups heavy cream
1 1/2 cups milk
1/4 cup sugar
1 tablespoon instant coffee granules
8 egg yolks

To prepare the whipped cream, beat the whipping cream, confectioners' sugar and vanilla in a mixing bowl until firm peaks form. Serve immediately or chill until serving time.

To prepare the custard cups, melt the chocolate with 1/2 cup of the cream in a 2-quart saucepan. Remove from the heat and set aside. Heat the remaining 1 cup cream, the milk, sugar and coffee granules in a saucepan until the sugar dissolves. Whisk the egg yolks in a large bowl. Whisk in the warm cream mixture gradually. Pour through a strainer into the melted chocolate mixture, stirring constantly. Divide equally among six custard cups. Place 1 inch apart in a baking pan. Add enough water to the baking pan to reach under the lips of the custard cups. Bake at 300 degrees for 45 minutes or until just set around the edges. Do not overcook. The custard will continue to cook after you remove it from the oven and the chocolate will harden as it cools. Loosely cover the custard cups and chill until serving time.

To serve, uncover the custard cups and dollop with the whipped cream. Garnish with sprigs of fresh mint.

Serves 6

Each day provides its own gifts.

—MARTIAL

Key Lime Pie Parfaits

1/2 cup fresh Key lime juice
1/4 teaspoon lime zest
1/4 cup sugar
1 (14-ounce) can sweetened
    condensed milk

2 eggs
1 1/2 cups Sweetened Whipped Cream
    (page 155)
1 cup graham cracker crumbs

Whisk the first five ingredients in a double boiler until smooth. Cook over simmering water for 6 minutes or until thickened, or to 160 degrees on a candy thermometer, stirring constantly. Set in ice in a large bowl for 20 minutes or until cool, stirring occasionally. Layer 1 tablespoon of the whipped cream, 1 tablespoon of the crumbs and 3 tablespoons of the lime mixture in each of eight 8-ounce parfait glasses. Repeat the layers once and top each with the remaining whipped cream. Garnish with additional Key lime zest.

Serves 8

A hero is a man who does what he can.

—ROMAIN ROLLAND

Marinated Fruit in Watermelon

1 cup raspberry sherbet
1 cup pineapple sherbet
1 cup mint sherbet
1 cup tangerine sherbet
1 watermelon

2 cantaloupes
2 fresh peaches, sliced
3 fresh plums, sliced
1 box fresh Louisiana strawberries
1 cup Cointreau

Scoop the sherbet into balls. Freeze for 8 to 10 hours. Cut the watermelon and scoop out the fruit with a melon baller, reserving the shell. Cut the reserved shell into an attractive design to hold the fruit. Cut the cantaloupes and scoop out the fruit with a melon baller. Macerate the fruit in the Cointreau in a bowl. Place the watermelon shell on a bed of crushed ice. Add the fruit and sherbet balls.

Serves 12

When you dig another out of their troubles, you find a place to bury your own.

—ANONYMOUS

Fat Tuesday Spiked Strawberries with French Vanilla Ice Cream

1 cup red port
1 cup burgundy
1/2 orange, sliced
1 lime, sliced
1 whole clove
1 cinnamon stick
1/2 cup packed light brown sugar
1 cup heavy whipping cream
1/4 cup granulated sugar
1 teaspoon vanilla extract
4 cups sliced fresh Louisiana strawberries
3 cups French vanilla ice cream

Bring the port and wine to a boil in a medium saucepan over medium-high heat. Add the orange slices, lime slices, clove, cinnamon stick and brown sugar. Return to a boil. Remove from the heat. Let cool for 30 minutes or longer. Strain into a bowl, discarding the solids. Chill, covered, for up to 2 weeks.

Whip the whipping cream in a bowl until soft peaks form. Add the granulated sugar and vanilla and beat until firm peaks form.

To serve, reserve 1 cup of the sliced strawberries for garnish. Place one scoop of ice cream in each of six Champagne flutes. Cover with the remaining strawberries and drizzle generously with the port sauce. Add a dollop of the whipped cream. Garnish with the reserved strawberries and sprigs of fresh mint.

Serves 6

*I am a great believer in luck, and I find the harder
I work, the more I have of it.*

—THOMAS JEFFERSON

The King's Cake

1 1/2 envelopes dry yeast
1 teaspoon sugar
1/3 cup warm water
4 cups all-purpose flour
1/2 teaspoon salt
2 tablespoons orange zest
1 cup (2 sticks) butter, softened
2/3 cup sugar
5 egg yolks
1/2 cup buttermilk

1 teaspoon vanilla extract
1 ounce Frangelica (hazelnut liqueur)
Cinnamon to taste
1 plastic king cake baby (see Note)
1 egg
1 tablespoon milk
1/2 cup sugar
Blue, red, green and yellow
    food coloring

Dissolve the yeast and 1 teaspoon sugar in the water in a bowl. Let stand until the mixture foams. Add one-third of the flour and mix to form a soft dough. Stir the salt and orange zest into the remaining flour.

Beat the butter and 2/3 cup sugar in a mixing bowl until creamy. Beat in 5 egg yolks one at a time, scraping down the side of the bowl once or twice. Add the buttermilk, vanilla and 1 ounce liqueur. Add the soft dough and enough of the orange flour mixture to form a firm dough. If the dough is too dry, add a small amount of water. Shape into a ball. Place in a greased bowl, turning to coat the surface. Cover with a damp cloth. Let rise for 2 hours or until doubled in bulk. Punch the dough down. Divide into three equal portions. Roll each portion into a rope 2 feet long on a lightly floured surface. Braid the ropes loosely, staggering the ends. Shape the braid into a circle and braid the ends together or wet the ends with a small amount of water and tie together. Dust lightly with cinnamon. Insert the plastic baby into the loaf to cover. Place on a greased baking sheet. Cover with a damp cloth and let rise in a warm place for 30 minutes. Brush with a mixture of 1 egg and 1 tablespoon milk. Bake at 375 degrees for 30 minutes or until golden brown. Brush with additional liqueur, if desired. Let stand to cool.

Divide 1/2 cup sugar among three small jars with lids. Tint one portion of the sugar purple by mixing with 1 drop of blue food coloring and 2 drops of red food coloring. Tint the remaining sugar portions with green food coloring and yellow food coloring. Decorate the loaf with alternating broad stripes of the tinted sugar or the design of choice. (Note: To prevent a choking hazard, place the plastic baby on top of the loaf after baking.)

Serves 8 to 9

A crown is merely a hat that lets the rain in.

—KING FREDERICK THE GREAT

The Queen's Cake

2/3 cup skinned hazelnuts, toasted
1 1/2 cups whipped topping
8 ounces cream cheese, softened
1 cup ground almonds
3/4 cup confectioners' sugar
1/4 cup candied citrus peel (see Note)
1 (17-ounce) package frozen puff pastry, thawed
1 egg, lightly beaten

Finely grind the hazelnuts in a food processor. Add the whipped topping, cream cheese, almonds, confectioners' sugar and citrus peel and blend well. Spoon into a bowl. Chill, covered, for 1 hour.

Cut each sheet of puff pastry into a 14-inch square on a lightly floured surface. Cut each square into a 12-inch circle using a plate as a guide, discarding the trimmings. Place each circle on a baking sheet. Cover with plastic wrap and chill until needed.

Uncover the pastry circles. Spoon the hazelnut mixture in the center of one of the circles, carefully spreading to 1 inch from the edge. Brush the rim with some of the egg. Cover with the remaining pastry circle and press the edges together to seal. Use a sharp knife or pizza cutter to neatly trim the edge of the pastry. Cut a hole in the top to allow the steam to escape. Brush with the remaining egg. Bake at 400 degrees for 35 minutes or until golden brown. Let cool completely before cutting into wedges to serve. Garnish with fresh Louisiana strawberries. *(Note: Candied citrus peel can be found in the baking section of your favorite grocery, or you can substitute the grated peel of one orange instead. To easily cut a pastry circle, place an inverted bowl on the pastry and use a sharp knife to cut around the bowl.)*

Serves 10

Even when freshly washed and relieved of all obvious confections,
children tend to be sticky.

—FRAN LEBOWITZ

Contraband Carrot Cake

Cake

3 cups all-purpose flour
1 1/2 cups sugar
1 teaspoon salt
1 tablespoon baking soda
1 tablespoon cinnamon
1 1/2 cups vegetable oil
4 eggs, lightly beaten
1 tablespoon vanilla extract
1 1/2 cups walnuts or nuts of
   choice, chopped

1 1/2 cups shredded coconut
2 cups shredded carrots
1 cup drained crushed pineapple

Lemon Cream Cheese Frosting

8 ounces cream cheese, softened
6 tablespoons unsalted
   butter, softened
2 1/2 cups confectioners' sugar
1 teaspoon vanilla extract
Juice of 1/2 lemon

To prepare the cake, sift the flour, sugar, salt, baking soda and cinnamon into a mixing bowl. Add the oil, eggs and vanilla and beat well. Fold in the walnuts, coconut, carrots and pineapple. Pour into two greased 9-inch cake pans. Bake at 350 degrees on the middle oven rack for 50 minutes or until the edges pull away from the side of the pans and a wooden pick inserted in the center comes out clean. Cool on wire racks.

To prepare the frosting, beat the cream cheese and butter in a mixing bowl until creamy. Add the confectioners' sugar gradually, beating constantly. Stir in the vanilla and lemon juice. Spread between the layers and over the top and side of the cake. Garnish the top with additional chopped walnuts or nuts of choice.

Serves 8 to 10

Be faithful in small things because it is in them that your strength lies.
—MOTHER TERESA

Old-Fashioned Chocolate Soda Pop Cake

Cake

2 cups sugar
2 cups all-purpose flour
1/2 teaspoon salt
1 cup cola
1/2 cup vegetable oil
1/2 cup (1 stick) butter
3 tablespoons baking cocoa
2 eggs
1/2 cup buttermilk
1 teaspoon baking soda
1 teaspoon vanilla extract

Chocolate Icing

1/2 cup (1 stick) butter
3 tablespoons baking cocoa
6 tablespoons cream or milk
1 teaspoon vanilla extract
1 (1-pound) package
  confectioners' sugar
1/2 to 1 cup pecans, chopped

To prepare the cake, mix the sugar, flour and salt together. Bring the cola, oil, butter and baking cocoa to a boil in a saucepan. Pour into a mixing bowl. Add the flour mixture and beat well. Add the eggs, buttermilk, baking soda and vanilla and mix well. Pour into a greased and floured 9×13-inch cake pan. Bake at 350 degrees for 20 to 25 minutes or until a wooden pick inserted in the center comes out clean.

To prepare the icing, heat the butter, baking cocoa and cream in a saucepan until the butter melts. Add the vanilla and confectioners' sugar and beat well. Stir in the pecans. Spread over the hot cake. Let stand until cool before serving.

Serves 10 to 12

Self-trust is the first secret of success.

—Anonymous

Chocolate Christmas Cake with Peppermints

Cake

1³/4 cups boiling water

1¹/2 cups baking cocoa

4 ounces bittersweet
    chocolate, chopped

1 cup buttermilk,
    at room temperature

1 tablespoon vanilla extract

3 cups cake flour

2¹/2 teaspoons baking soda

1 teaspoon salt

2 cups (4 sticks) unsalted
    butter, softened

1¹/2 cups granulated sugar

1¹/2 cups packed dark brown sugar

4 eggs, at room temperature

Chocolate Glaze

1¹/4 cups heavy cream

12 ounces bittersweet
    chocolate, chopped

2 tablespoons unsalted butter, softened

Peppermint Filling

2 ounces whole round
    peppermint candies

1 cup confectioners' sugar

12 ounces whipped cream cheese,
    at room temperature

¹/4 cup unsalted butter, softened

2 teaspoons vanilla extract

Assembly

¹/2 cup chopped round
    peppermint candies

To prepare the cake, arrange the oven racks in the upper and lower thirds of the oven. Butter three 9-inch cake pans and line the bottoms with baking parchment or waxed paper. Butter the baking parchment and sprinkle with cake flour, tapping out the excess. Whisk the boiling water into the baking cocoa in a heat-proof bowl until smooth. Add the bittersweet chocolate. Let stand for 1 minute and then whisk until smooth. Let cool for 5 minutes. Whisk in the buttermilk and vanilla. Whisk the cake flour, baking soda and salt in a bowl. Beat the butter, granulated sugar and brown sugar at medium speed in a large mixing bowl for 4 minutes or until light and fluffy. Add the eggs one at a time, beating well and scraping down the side of the bowl with a spatula after each addition. Add the cake flour mixture and chocolate mixture alternately, beating at low speed until just combined and beginning and ending with the cake flour mixture. Divide the batter equally among the prepared pans, smoothing the tops. Bake at 350 degrees for 40 to 45 minutes or until a wooden pick inserted in the center comes out with a few crumbs clinging to it and the layers begin to pull away from the sides of the pans. Cool in the pans for 5 minutes. Loosen each layer from the side of the pan and invert onto wire racks. Peel off the baking parchment and invert the layers again so they are right side up. Cool completely.

To prepare the glaze, bring the cream to a simmer in a small saucepan over medium heat. Remove from the heat. Add the bittersweet chocolate and butter. Stir for 5 minutes or until smooth. Spoon into a bowl. Let cool for 15 minutes.

To prepare the filling, pulse the peppermint candies and confectioners' sugar in a food processor until finely ground. Combine with the cream cheese, butter and vanilla in a bowl and mix well.

To assemble, place one cake layer on an 8-inch cardboard round on an 8-inch round wire rack. Spread with one-half of the filling and top with another cake layer right side up. Spread with the remaining filling and top with the remaining cake layer right side up. Place the layers on a rack in a baking pan. Pour some of the glaze over the top, smoothing onto the side with a small metal spatula. Continue to pour and spread the remaining glaze over the cake until the cake is evenly coated, using simple even strokes and the drippings in the pan if needed. Chill on the rack for 15 minutes or until the glaze is just set. Sprinkle the chopped candies around the edge of the cake. Place the cake on a cake stand or cake plate. Bring to room temperature before serving.

Serves 12

Happiness lies in the joy of achievement and the thrill of creative effort.
—Franklin D. Roosevelt

Café au Lait Chocolate Walnut Cake

Cake

10 ounces ground walnuts
$1/3$ cup all-purpose flour
2 teaspoons cornstarch
1 teaspoon baking powder
12 egg whites
$1/4$ teaspoon salt
12 egg yolks
$1^1/4$ cups sugar
2 teaspoons vanilla extract

Mocha Frosting

6 ounces unsweetened chocolate
$3/4$ cup ($1^1/2$ sticks) unsalted
   butter, softened
$1^1/2$ teaspoons vanilla extract
$1^1/4$ cups confectioners' sugar, sifted
$3/4$ cup brewed strong dark roast coffee
$1^1/2$ tablespoons coffee liqueur
$4^1/2$ cups confectioners' sugar, sifted

Coffee Cream

2 cups heavy whipping cream
2 teaspoons instant coffee granules
$1/4$ cup confectioners' sugar
$1/4$ cup chopped walnuts

To prepare the cake, lightly coat two 10-inch cake pans with butter. Line the bottoms with baking parchment and grease with butter. Mix the walnuts, flour, cornstarch and baking powder in a bowl. Beat the egg whites and salt at medium-high speed in a mixing bowl until stiff. Beat the egg yolks at medium-high speed in a large mixing bowl until pale yellow. Add the sugar gradually, beating for 5 minutes or until fluffy. Add the vanilla. Sprinkle with the walnut mixture and fold in the egg whites. Spoon into the prepared pans. Bake at 350 degrees for 25 to 30 minutes or until the centers spring back when lightly touched. Invert onto wire racks to cool completely.

To prepare the frosting, melt the chocolate in a heatproof bowl over 1 inch of just simmering water, stirring occasionally. Beat the butter, melted chocolate, vanilla and $1^1/4$ cups confectioners' sugar in a mixing bowl until creamy. Add the coffee, liqueur and $4^1/2$ cups confectioners' sugar alternately, beating until fluffy.

To prepare the cream, beat the first three ingredients in a mixing bowl until soft peaks form. Split the cake layers horizontally with a serrated knife. Place one layer on a cake plate and spread with $3/4$ cup of the frosting and one-third of the coffee cream. Repeat the layers twice. Top with the remaining cake layer. Spread the remaining frosting over the top and side of the cake. Sprinkle with the walnuts. Chill until serving time.

Serves 18

People often say that motivation doesn't last. Well, neither does bathing.
That's why we recommend it daily.

—ZIG ZIGLAR

John-Allen's German Chocolate Cake with Bourbon Pecans

Cake
4 ounces sweet baking chocolate
1/2 cup boiling water
2 1/2 cups sifted cake flour
1 teaspoon baking soda
1/2 teaspoon salt
1 cup (2 sticks) butter, softened
2 cups sugar
4 egg yolks
1 teaspoon vanilla extract
1 cup buttermilk
4 egg whites, stiffly beaten

Coconut Pecan Frosting
1 cup evaporated milk
1 cup sugar
3 egg yolks
1/2 cup (1 stick) butter
1 teaspoon vanilla extract
1 1/3 cups flaked coconut
1 cup chopped Bourbon Pecans
  (page 181) or pecans

To prepare the cake, melt the chocolate in the boiling water and let stand until cool. Sift the cake flour, baking soda and salt together. Cream the butter and sugar in a mixing bowl until light and fluffy. Add the egg yolks one at a time, beating well after each addition. Add the melted chocolate and vanilla and mix well. Add the flour mixture and buttermilk alternately, beating until smooth after each addition. Fold in the egg whites. Spoon into three 9-inch cake pans lined with waxed paper. Bake at 350 degrees for 30 to 40 minutes or until the layers test done. Cool slightly in the pans and invert onto wire racks to cool.

To prepare the frosting, combine the evaporated milk, sugar, egg yolks, butter and vanilla in a saucepan. Cook over medium heat for 12 minutes or until thickened, stirring constantly. Add the coconut and bourbon pecans and beat until cool and of spreading consistency. Spread between the layers and over the top and side of the cake.

Serves 8 to 10

If you've had a good time playing the game,
you're a winner even if you lose.

—MALCOLM FORBES

Ragin' Cajun Red Velvet Cake

Cake

3 cups vegetable oil

3 1/2 cups sugar

6 eggs

2 cups buttermilk

8 ounces semisweet chocolate, grated

5 cups all-purpose flour or cake flour

2 teaspoons vanilla extract

1 tablespoon baking soda

2 teaspoons salt

1 tablespoon white vinegar

1 (3-ounce) bottle red food coloring

Cream Cheese Frosting

24 ounces cream cheese, softened

2 cups (4 sticks) unsalted
    butter, softened

6 cups confectioners' sugar

2 teaspoons vanilla extract

Chopped pecans, finely chopped
    peppermint or shredded sweetened
    or unsweetened coconut

To prepare the cake, whisk the oil, sugar and eggs in a mixing bowl until smooth. Whisk in the buttermilk, chocolate, flour, vanilla, baking soda and salt until blended. Add the vinegar and mix well. Stir in the food coloring. Divide evenly among six 9-inch cake pans coated with nonstick baking spray. Bake at 350 degrees evenly spaced apart for 15 minutes or until the layers pull away from the sides of the pans and a wooden pick inserted in the center comes out clean, rotating the pans halfway through baking. Do not overbake.

To prepare the frosting, beat the cream cheese, butter and confectioners' sugar at low speed in a mixing bowl until mixed. Beat at high speed for 5 minutes or until light and fluffy, scraping down the side of the bowl with a rubber spatula halfway through the beating process. Reduce the speed to low and beat in the vanilla. Increase the speed to high and continue beating until fluffy, scraping the bowl again if needed. Chill until slightly stiff. Spread between the layers and over the top and side of the cake. Sprinkle with chopped pecans. (*Note: The cake may be baked in three cake pans for thicker layers but increase the baking time to 30 minutes. The frosting may be stored in the refrigerator for 3 days. The chopped pecans may also be mixed into the frosting. Pecan halves may also be used as a garnish.*)

Serves 15 to 20

The really happy man is one who can enjoy the scenery on a detour.

—Anonymous

Gâteau de Fruit Tropical
(Cake of Tropical Fruit)

2 cups all-purpose flour
1 cup (2 sticks) butter, softened
1/2 cup packed brown sugar
1/2 cup pecans, chopped
8 ounces cream cheese, softened
1/2 cup (1 stick) butter, softened
1 (1-pound) package confectioners' sugar
4 or 5 bananas, sliced
1 (20-ounce) can crushed pineapple, drained
16 ounces whipped topping
Sliced fresh Louisiana strawberries

Combine the flour, 1 cup butter, the brown sugar and pecans in a bowl and mix well. Spread in a 9×13-inch baking pan. Bake at 350 degrees for 15 minutes. Let stand until cool. Reserve 1 cup of the pecan mixture for topping.

Beat the cream cheese, 1/2 cup butter and the confectioners' sugar in a mixing bowl until smooth. Spread over the baked layer. Layer the bananas, pineapple and whipped topping over the cream cheese layer. Sprinkle the reserved pecan mixture over the layers. Top with sliced strawberries. Chill for 4 hours before serving.

Serves 10 to 12

There is no failure, except in no longer trying.

—ELBERT HUBBARD

Brown Sugar Pound Cake

3 cups all-purpose flour
1/2 teaspoon baking powder
1/8 teaspoon salt
3/4 cup (1 1/2 sticks) unsalted butter, softened
3/4 cup shortening
2 1/4 cups packed brown sugar
5 egg yolks, well beaten
1 cup milk
1 cup chopped pecans
1 teaspoon vanilla extract
5 egg whites, stiffly beaten

Sift the flour, baking powder and salt together. Cream the butter, shortening and brown sugar in a mixing bowl until light and fluffy. Add the egg yolks and mix well. Add the flour mixture alternately with the milk, mixing well after each addition and ending with the flour mixture. Add the pecans and vanilla and mix well. Fold in the egg whites gently. Fill a greased and floured tube pan three-fourths full. Bake at 325 degrees for 1 1/2 hours. Cool slightly in the pan. Loosen the cake from the side of the pan and invert onto a serving plate.

Serves 12

One who walks the road with love will never walk the road alone.

—C. T. Davis

Grandma Gert's Buttermilk Pound Cake

3 cups cake flour
$1/4$ teaspoon baking soda
$1/2$ teaspoon salt
1 cup (2 sticks) butter, softened
3 cups sugar
6 eggs
2 teaspoons vanilla extract
1 cup buttermilk

Mix the cake flour, baking soda and salt together. Beat the butter and sugar in a mixing bowl until light and fluffy. Add the eggs one at a time, beating well after each addition. Stir in the vanilla. Add the flour mixture alternately with the buttermilk, mixing well after each addition. Pour into a greased 9- or 10-inch bundt pan. Bake at 325 degrees for $1^{1}/2$ hours or until the cake begins to pull away from the side of the pan. Do not open the oven door to check for doneness until after 1 hour. Cool in the pan for 10 minutes. Invert onto a wire rack to cool completely.

Serves 12 to 14

There is much to be said for failure. It is more interesting than success.

—MAX BEERBOHM

Baronnette Bars

8 cups cornflakes

2 cups peanuts

1 cup granulated sugar

1 cup packed brown sugar

1 1/2 cups light corn syrup

1 cup peanut butter

2 cups (12 ounces) semisweet
   chocolate chips

Mix the cornflakes and peanuts in a large bowl. Combine the granulated sugar, brown sugar and corn syrup in a saucepan. Heat over medium heat until melted, stirring constantly. Stir in the peanut butter. Pour over the cornflake mixture and mix until coated. Spoon into a 9×13-inch dish sprayed with nonstick cooking spray. Sprinkle the chocolate chips over the top. Bake at 200 degrees until the chocolate chips soften. Spread over the top. Let stand for several hours or until the chocolate hardens. Cut into small squares.

Makes 1 1/2 to 2 dozen

Children are the reward of life.

—CONGOLESE PROVERB

Award-Winning Brownies

4 ounces unsweetened chocolate

1/2 cup (1 stick) unsalted butter

1 1/4 cups plus 1 tablespoon sugar

1/2 teaspoon vanilla extract

3 eggs

3/4 cup all-purpose flour

3/4 cup chopped nuts

Melt the chocolate and butter in a saucepan, stirring constantly. Combine the chocolate mixture, sugar and vanilla in a bowl and mix well. Add the eggs one at a time, mixing well after each addition. Add the flour gradually, stirring constantly. Stir in the nuts. Pour into a buttered and floured 8×8-inch baking pan. Bake at 325 degrees for 35 minutes. Cool for 1 hour before cutting. For the best flavor, serve the following day.

Serves 9

You don't choose your family. They are God's gift to you, as you are to them.

—DESMOND TUTU

Café Liqueur Brownies

Brownies

$1/2$ cup all-purpose flour
1 cup quick-cooking oats
$1/2$ cup packed brown sugar
$1/3$ cup butter, melted
1 tablespoon instant coffee granules
$1/4$ teaspoon salt
$1/3$ cup butter
2 ounces unsweetened chocolate
2 eggs

1 cup sugar
2 tablespoons coffee liqueur
$3/4$ cup all-purpose flour
$3/4$ cup chopped nuts

Chocolate Frosting

$1/3$ cup butter
$2 1/4$ cups confectioners' sugar
$1 1/2$ tablespoons coffee liqueur
2 tablespoons chopped coffee beans

To prepare the brownies, mix $1/2$ cup flour, the oats, brown sugar, $1/3$ cup butter, the coffee granules and salt in a bowl. Press into a 9×9-inch baking pan. Bake at 350 degrees for 12 minutes. Maintain the oven temperature. Melt $1/3$ cup butter and the chocolate in a small saucepan over medium-low heat, stirring frequently. Remove from the heat and let cool. Beat the eggs at medium speed in a mixing bowl until thick and pale yellow. Beat in the sugar and liqueur. Stir in $3/4$ cup flour and the nuts. Spread over the crust. Bake for 25 minutes. Cool in the pan on a wire rack.

To prepare the frosting, cream the butter in a mixing bowl. Add the confectioners' sugar and liqueur gradually, beating constantly. Fold in the coffee beans. Spread over the cooled brownies. Cut into squares. Garnish with additional coffee beans.

Serves 16

The possibilities are unlimited as long as you are true to your life's purpose.

—Marcia Wieder

Buccaneer Bananas Foster Cookies

Cookies

3/4 cup packed dark brown sugar
3/4 cup (1 1/2 sticks) unsalted
    butter, softened
2/3 cup mashed bananas
1 egg
1/2 cup (3 ounces) cinnamon chips
1 teaspoon rum extract or
    vanilla extract
2 cups organic all-purpose flour
1/2 teaspoon baking powder
1/2 teaspoon baking soda
1/4 teaspoon salt

Cinnamon Glaze

1/4 cup (1/2 stick) unsalted butter
2 tablespoons brown sugar
1 tablespoon cinnamon chips
2 tablespoons half-and-half
1 cup confectioners' sugar
1/2 teaspoon rum extract or
    vanilla extract
1/4 cup walnuts

To prepare the cookies, cream the brown sugar and butter at medium speed in a large mixing bowl until light and fluffy, scraping the side of the bowl frequently. Add the bananas, egg, cinnamon chips and rum extract and beat until blended. Reduce the speed to low and beat in the flour, baking powder, baking soda and salt. Drop by rounded tablespoonfuls 2 inches apart onto ungreased cookie sheets. Bake at 350 degrees for 10 to 12 minutes or until the edges are light brown. Cool completely on a wire rack.

To prepare the glaze, melt the butter in a small saucepan over medium-low heat. Add the brown sugar, cinnamon chips and half-and-half. Bring to a boil, stirring constantly. Remove from the heat. Add the confectioners' sugar and rum extract and beat at medium speed until blended. Spread over the cooled cookies. Place the walnuts in a small grater and grate over the top of each cookie.

Makes 2 1/2 dozen

Pretty much all the honest truth telling there is
in the world is done by children.

—OLIVER WENDELL HOLMES, SR.

Chocolate Mocha Toffee Cookies

1 cup all-purpose flour
1/2 cup Dutch-process baking cocoa
1 teaspoon baking cocoa
1/4 teaspoon salt
1/2 cup (1 stick) unsalted butter, softened
3/4 cup sugar
1 egg
1 teaspoon vanilla extract
1/2 cup Heath bites candy, cut into halves
1/2 cup chocolate-covered coffee beans, cut into halves
1/2 cup walnuts, toasted and coarsely chopped

Arrange the oven racks in the upper and lower thirds of the oven. Line two cookie sheets with baking parchment. Sift the flour, Dutch-process baking cocoa, baking cocoa and salt together. Cream the butter and sugar at high speed in a large mixing bowl for 2 minutes or until light and fluffy. Add the eggs and vanilla and mix well. Reduce the speed to low and beat in the flour mixture gradually. Fold in the Heath bites, coffee beans and walnuts. Drop by 1 1/2-inch ice cream scoopfuls 2 inches apart onto the prepared cookie sheets. Bake at 350 degrees for 12 minutes or until set, switching the cookie sheets between the oven racks halfway through the baking time. Do not overbake. Cool on the cookie sheets for 5 minutes. Remove to wire racks to cool completely.

Makes 2 dozen

Your goal should be out of reach but not out of sight.
—ANITA DeFRANTZ

"Geaux Tigers"
Granola and Cranberry Chocolate Chip Cookies

1 cup all-purpose flour
1/2 teaspoon baking soda
1/4 teaspoon baking powder
1/2 teaspoon salt
1/2 teaspoon cinnamon
1/2 teaspoon nutmeg
1/2 cup (1 stick) unsalted butter, softened
3/4 cup packed light brown sugar
1 egg
1/2 teaspoon vanilla extract
1 1/2 cups granola
1/4 cup dried cranberries, chopped
1 cup (6 ounces) semisweet chocolate chips

Whisk the flour, baking soda, baking powder, salt, cinnamon and nutmeg together in a bowl. Cream the butter and brown sugar at medium speed in a mixing bowl until light and fluffy. Beat in the egg and then the vanilla. Add the flour mixture and beat well. Stir in the granola, dried cranberries and chocolate chips. Drop by rounded tablespoonfuls 2 inches apart onto buttered cookie sheets. Bake in batches on the middle oven rack for 12 to 15 minutes or until golden brown. Cool on wire racks.

Makes 3 dozen

Don't brag; it isn't the whistle that pulls the train.
—ANONYMOUS

Cinnamon-Spice, Everything Nice
(A Cajun Girl's Cookies)

1 cup (2 sticks) butter, softened
1 1/2 cups sugar
3 eggs, beaten
2 1/2 cups all-purpose flour
1 teaspoon salt
1 1/2 teaspoons cinnamon
1 1/2 teaspoons ground allspice
1 teaspoon baking soda
1 tablespoon water
1 pound pecans, chopped
1 (15-ounce) package raisins (optional)

Cream the butter and sugar in a mixing bowl until light and fluffy. Add the eggs and mix well. Add the flour, salt, cinnamon and allspice and mix well. Dissolve the baking soda in the water. Stir into the batter. Stir in the pecans and raisins. Drop by spoonfuls onto greased cookie sheets. Bake at 350 degrees for 15 minutes or until brown. Cool on a wire rack.

Makes 2 1/2 dozen

You might be from Louisiana if…You don't learn until high school that Mardi Gras is not a national holiday.

—ANONYMOUS

Awesome Apple Pie

6 apples, peeled and sliced
1 tablespoon cornstarch
1/2 teaspoon salt
3 tablespoons butter, melted
1 teaspoon cinnamon
3 tablespoons granulated sugar
1/3 cup light corn syrup
2 homemade pie pastries
1/2 cup packed light brown sugar
3 tablespoons light corn syrup
1/4 cup nuts, chopped
2 tablespoons all-purpose flour
2 tablespoons butter, softened

Place the apples in a microwave-safe bowl. Microwave on High until slightly softened. Combine the cornstarch, salt, 3 tablespoons butter, the cinnamon, granulated sugar and 1/3 cup corn syrup in a bowl and mix well. Fit one of the pie pastries into a 9-inch deep-dish pie plate, fluting the edge. Fill with the apples. Pour the corn syrup mixture over the apples. Cut the remaining pie pastry into strips. Arrange lattice-fashion over the pie. Cover the edge with foil to prevent overbrowning. Bake at 400 degrees for 30 to 45 minutes or until cooked through.

Mix the brown sugar, 3 tablespoons corn syrup, the nuts, flour and 2 tablespoons butter in a bowl. Remove the pie from the oven and discard the foil. Spread the brown sugar mixture over the crust. Return to the oven and bake for 10 minutes or until bubbly.

Serves 8

The ornament of a house is the friends who frequent it.

—RALPH WALDO EMERSON

MeMaw's Chocolate Meringue Pie

Pie

3/4 cup sugar
5 tablespoons baking cocoa
3 tablespoons cornstarch
1/2 teaspoon salt
3 cups milk
3 egg yolks, beaten
1 teaspoon vanilla extract
1 baked (9-inch) pie shell

Meringue

3 egg whites, at room temperature
1/4 teaspoon cream of tartar
6 tablespoons sugar

To prepare the pie, mix the sugar, baking cocoa, cornstarch and salt in a heavy saucepan. Add the milk gradually. Cook over medium heat until thickened and bubbly, stirring constantly. Reduce the heat. Cook for 2 minutes longer, stirring constantly. Remove from the heat. Stir about 1 cup of the hot filling into the egg yolks. Stir the egg yolks into the remaining hot filling. Bring to a gentle boil. Cook for 2 minutes, stirring constantly. Remove from the heat. Stir in the vanilla. Pour into the baked pie shell.

To prepare the meringue, beat the egg whites and cream of tartar in a mixing bowl until soft peaks form. Add the sugar gradually, beating constantly at high speed until stiff peaks form. Spread over the warm filling, sealing to the edge and using the back of a spoon to make swirls and peaks on top. Bake at 350 degrees for 15 minutes or until golden brown. (*Note: The entire top of the pie does not have to be golden brown.*)

Serves 8

Believe and act as if it were impossible to fail.

—CHARLES F. KETTERING

Carnival Coconut Cream Pie

1 refrigerator pie pastry
$1/2$ cup sugar
$1/4$ cup cornstarch
2 cups half-and-half
4 egg yolks
3 tablespoons butter
1 cup sweetened flaked coconut
1 teaspoon vanilla extract
2 cups heavy whipping cream
$1/3$ cup sugar
$1^1/2$ teaspoons vanilla extract
1 cup sweetened flaked coconut, toasted

Fit the pie pastry into a 9-inch pie plate, fluting the edge. Prick the bottom and side with a fork. Bake using the package directions. Mix $1/2$ cup sugar and the cornstarch in a heavy saucepan. Whisk the half-and-half and egg yolks in a bowl. Whisk the egg mixture into the sugar mixture. Bring to a boil over medium heat, whisking constantly. Boil for 1 minute. Remove from the heat. Stir in the butter, 1 cup coconut and 1 teaspoon vanilla. Cover the surface with plastic wrap. Let stand for 30 minutes. Remove the plastic wrap and spoon the coconut mixture into the baked pie shell. Cover and chill for 30 minutes or until set.

Beat the whipping cream at high speed in a mixing bowl until foamy. Add $1/3$ cup sugar and $1^1/2$ teaspoons vanilla gradually, beating until firm peaks form. Spread over the top of the pie. Sprinkle with the toasted coconut.

Serves 6 to 8

A kindergarten teacher is a person who knows how to make little things count.

—ANONYMOUS

Gator-on-the-Geaux Cream Pie

1¹/4 cups chocolate wafer crumbs
¹/4 cup sugar
¹/3 cup melted butter
1 envelope unflavored gelatin
¹/4 cup sugar
¹/8 teaspoon salt
¹/2 cup cold water
3 egg yolks
¹/4 cup green crème de menthe
¹/4 cup crème de cacao
3 egg whites, at room temperature
¹/4 cup sugar
1 cup heavy whipping cream, whipped

Mix the wafer crumbs, ¹/4 cup sugar and the butter in a bowl. Press over the bottom and up the side of a 9-inch pie plate. Bake at 400 degrees for 5 minutes. Remove from the oven to cool.

Combine the gelatin, ¹/4 cup sugar, the salt and cold water in a saucepan. Let stand until the gelatin softens. Add the egg yolks one at a time, beating well after each addition. Cook over low heat for 3 to 5 minutes or until the gelatin dissolves and the mixture thickens slightly, stirring constantly. Remove from the heat. Stir in the crème de menthe and crème de cacao. Chill until the mixture is the consistency of unbeaten egg whites, stirring occasionally.

Beat the egg whites in a mixing bowl until stiff but not dry. Add ¹/4 cup sugar gradually, beating until very stiff. Fold into the gelatin mixture. Fold in the whipped cream. Spoon into the cooled piecrust. Chill for 2 to 10 hours. Garnish with additional whipped cream and shaved chocolate.

Serves 8

To make your children capable of honesty is the beginning of education.

—JOHN RUSKIN

Luscious Lemon Meringue Pie

Pie
7 tablespoons cornstarch
1 1/2 cups sugar
1/4 teaspoon salt
1 1/2 cups hot water
3 egg yolks
2 tablespoons grated lemon zest
1/2 cup lemon juice
3 tablespoons unsalted butter
1 baked (9-inch) pie shell

Meringue
3 egg whites, at room temperature
1/4 teaspoon cream of tartar
6 tablespoons sugar

To prepare the pie, mix the cornstarch, sugar, salt and hot water in a saucepan. Cook over medium heat for 6 minutes or until the mixture is thick and translucent, stirring constantly. Remove from the heat. Add a small amount of the hot mixture to the egg yolks. Stir the egg yolks into the hot mixture. Cook over low heat for 6 minutes, stirring constantly. Stir in the lemon zest, lemon juice and butter. Pour into the baked pie shell.

To prepare the meringue, beat the egg whites and cream of tartar in a mixing bowl until soft peaks form. Add the sugar gradually, beating at high speed until stiff peaks form. Spread over the pie, sealing to the edge and using the back of a spoon to make swirls and peaks on top. Bake at 350 degrees for 15 minutes or until golden brown. (Note: The entire top of the pie does not have to be golden brown.)

Serves 8

Children require guidance and sympathy far more than instruction.
—ANN SULLIVAN

Pirate's Peach Pie with Rum Pecans

Rum or Bourbon Pecans
1 pound pecan halves
2 cups rum or bourbon
1 cup sugar

Pie
1/4 cup (1/2 stick) butter, softened
1/4 cup granulated sugar
2 tablespoons all-purpose flour

1/4 teaspoon salt
1/2 cup light corn syrup
3 eggs
1 1/2 cups chopped fresh peaches
1 unbaked (9-inch) pie shell
1/4 cup all-purpose flour
1/4 cup packed brown sugar
2 tablespoons butter, softened

To prepare the pecans, layer the pecans in a shallow glass dish. Cover with the rum. Cover the dish loosely with plastic wrap and weigh down with dried beans to keep the pecans submerged. Let soak in the refrigerator for 3 days or longer. Remove the pecans from the rum. Toss the pecans in the sugar in a bowl. Spread the pecans on sheets of waxed paper to air dry for 2 to 3 hours or until the sugar crystallizes slightly. Pour the remaining rum into the nearest shot glass and sit for a spell, sipping slowly while the pecans air dry. However, we do not recommend sipping that long. Be sure to savor that nice nutty flavor. Chop 1/2 cup of the rum pecans to use in the pie. Reserve the remaining pecans for another purpose.

To prepare the pie, cream 1/4 cup butter, the granulated sugar and 2 tablespoons flour in a mixing bowl. Stir in the salt and corn syrup. Beat in the eggs one at a time, beating until blended after each addition. Stir in the peaches. Pour into the pie shell. Mix 1/4 cup flour and the brown sugar in a bowl. Add 2 tablespoons butter and the chopped rum pecans and mix well. Sprinkle over the top of the pie. Bake at 375 degrees for 35 to 40 minutes or until a knife inserted in the center comes out clean. (*Note: To prepare Chocolate-Dipped Rum Pecans, dip the remaining rum pecans in 2 cups semisweet chocolate chips, melted, and place on sheets of waxed paper to dry. This makes a great gift or decadent treat for yourself.*)

Serves 8

You can never consent to creep when one feels an impulse to soar.

—HELEN KELLER

Strawberry Patch Pie with a Punch

1 (13-ounce) package graham cracker crumbs
1/2 gallon premium strawberry ice cream
16 ounces fresh Louisiana strawberries
1/2 cup confectioners' sugar
1 (6-ounce) can frozen limeade concentrate, partially thawed
1/2 cup tequila
1/4 cup orange liqueur

Prepare a crust from the graham cracker crumbs using the package directions. Press the mixture firmly over the bottom of a lightly greased 10-inch springform pan. Let the ice cream stand at room temperature for 20 minutes or until slightly softened. Process the strawberries and confectioners' sugar in a food processor until puréed, stopping to scrape down the side as needed.

Place the ice cream in a large bowl and cut into 3-inch pieces. Fold in the strawberry mixture, limeade concentrate, tequila and orange liqueur until blended. Spoon into the crust in the springform pan. Freeze for 3 hours or until firm. Let stand at room temperature for 10 minutes before serving. Release the side of the pan and garnish with lime curls, whole strawberries and pretzels. (*Note: The pie will soften quickly due to the alcohol content, which lowers the freezing temperature of the ice cream. For variation, omit the tequila and orange liqueur and add one 6-ounce can frozen orange juice concentrate, partially thawed. Proceed with the recipe as directed. Let stand at room temperature for 15 minutes before serving.*)

Serves 10 to 12

Lost time is never found again.
—BENJAMIN FRANKLIN

Lagniappe

EASY PLAY DOUGH

1 cup all-purpose flour
1 cup salt
1 tablespoon cream of tartar
1 tablespoon vegetable oil
1 cup water
Food coloring
1/4 teaspoon peppermint extract

Combine the flour, salt, cream of tartar, oil, water, food coloring and peppermint extract in a saucepan and mix well.

Cook the mixture over medium heat for 3 to 5 minutes or until the mixture forms a ball, stirring constantly. Remove from the heat to cool.

Knead the cooled mixture until smooth. Divide into balls and store in airtight containers.

NOTE: *This recipe will make 2 cups of dough.*

Cheesy Biscuits

2 cups all-purpose flour
1 tablespoon baking powder
1 tablespoon sugar
1/2 teaspoon salt
1 1/4 cups (5 ounces) shredded Cheddar cheese
1/4 cup (1/2 stick) cold butter, shredded
3/4 cup milk

Place a 12-inch Dutch oven on twelve hot coals. Place the lid on the Dutch oven and place twenty hot coals on the lid. Preheat for 10 minutes. Mix the flour, baking powder, sugar and salt in a bowl. Stir in the cheese and butter. Add the milk and stir with a fork until moistened. Knead on a lightly floured surface two to four times. Pat or roll the dough 1/2 inch thick. Cut with a floured 2-inch cutter. Place in the preheated Dutch oven. Cover and bake for 12 to 15 minutes or until cooked through. (*Note: You may place the biscuits on a greased baking sheet and bake at 450 degrees for 10 to 12 minutes or until golden brown. To use non-shredded butter, cut the butter into the flour mixture with a pastry blender until the mixture resembles coarse crumbs and then stir in the cheese.*)

Serves 15 to 18

Keep your promises to yourself.
—DAVID HAROLD FINK

Corn Festival Corn Bread

2 ears fresh corn
$1^1/2$ teaspoons vegetable oil
1 tablespoon butter
$^1/2$ cup 2% milk
$1^1/2$ tablespoons vegetable oil
$1^1/4$ cups 2% milk
1 egg, lightly beaten

1 egg white, lightly beaten
$1^1/2$ cups yellow cornmeal
1 cup all-purpose flour
$^1/4$ cup sugar
1 tablespoon baking powder
1 teaspoon salt

Remove the husks and silk from the corn. Using a sharp knife, cut the kernels into a bowl. Scrape the ears with a knife to release the liquid. Coat a 10-inch cast-iron skillet with $1^1/2$ teaspoons oil. Heat in a 400-degree oven for 10 minutes.

Melt the butter in a nonstick skillet over medium-high heat. Add the corn. Sauté for 2 minutes and remove from the heat. Process one-half of the corn and $^1/2$ cup milk in a blender until smooth. Combine the puréed corn mixture and sautéed corn in a medium bowl. Add $1^1/2$ tablespoons oil, $1^1/4$ cups milk, the egg and egg white and mix well.

Mix the cornmeal, flour, sugar, baking powder and salt in a large bowl. Make a well in the center and add the corn mixture, stirring just until moist. Pour into the preheated skillet. Bake at 400 degrees for 25 minutes or until a wooden pick inserted near the center comes out clean.

Serves 8 to 12

The child must know that he is a miracle, that since the beginning of the world there hasn't been and until the end of the world there will not be, another child like him.

—PABLO CASALS

Granny Annie's "Blue Ribbon" Blueberry Bread

Bread

2 cups all-purpose flour
1 cup sugar
2¹/2 teaspoons baking powder
1/2 teaspoon salt
1 egg
1 cup milk
3 tablespoons vegetable oil
1 cup fresh or frozen blueberries

Vanilla Sauce

1 cup sugar
1 cup cornstarch
1 cup heavy whipping cream
1/2 cup (1 stick) butter, cut into cubes

To prepare the bread, mix the flour, sugar, baking powder and salt in a bowl. Beat the egg, milk and oil in a large mixing bowl until smooth. Add the flour mixture gradually, beating until just combined after each addition. Fold in the blueberries. Pour into a greased 5×8-inch loaf pan. Bake at 350 degrees for 50 to 55 minutes or until the loaf tests done. Cool in the pan for 10 minutes. Remove to a wire rack to cool completely.

To prepare the sauce, mix the sugar and cornstarch in a saucepan. Stir in the cream until smooth. Add the butter. Bring to a boil over medium heat. Boil for 2 minutes, stirring constantly. Serve warm over the bread.

Makes 1 loaf

It may be face powder that gets a man, but it is
baking powder that keeps him.

—ANONYMOUS

Harvest Pumpkin Bread

3 1/2 cups all-purpose flour
3 cups sugar
1 1/2 teaspoons salt
2 teaspoons baking soda
1 teaspoon nutmeg
1 1/2 teaspoons cinnamon
4 eggs
1 cup vegetable oil
1/2 teaspoon vanilla extract
2/3 cup water
1 (15-ounce) can pumpkin

Mix the flour, sugar, salt, baking soda, nutmeg and cinnamon in a large bowl.
Combine the eggs, oil, vanilla, water and pumpkin in a bowl and mix well. Stir into
the flour mixture. Pour into four to six miniature loaf pans. Bake at 350 degrees for
30 to 40 minutes or until a wooden pick inserted in the center comes out clean.
Cool on a wire rack.

Makes 4 to 6 miniature loaves

*Children are one-third of our population
and all of our future.*

—SELECT PANEL FOR THE PROMOTION OF CHILD HEALTH, 1981

Zydeco Zucchini Bread

3 cups all-purpose flour
1 teaspoon salt
1 teaspoon baking soda
1 tablespoon cinnamon
1/4 teaspoon baking powder
3 eggs
2 cups sugar
1 cup vegetable oil
2 cups grated zucchini
1 cup walnuts, chopped (optional)

Sift the flour, salt, baking soda, cinnamon and baking powder together. Beat the eggs in a mixing bowl until light. Add the sugar, oil, zucchini and walnuts and beat well. Add the flour mixture and mix well. Spoon into two greased 4×8-inch loaf pans. Bake at 325 degrees for 1 hour or until the loaves test done. Cool on a wire rack.

Makes 2 loaves

Find something you're passionate about and keep tremendously interested in it.

—JULIA CHILD

Buttermilk Rolls

1 cup lukewarm buttermilk
1/4 teaspoon baking soda
1 teaspoon sugar
1 teaspoon salt
1 envelope dry yeast
3 tablespoons shortening
2 1/2 to 2 3/4 cups sifted all-purpose flour

Combine the buttermilk, baking soda, sugar and salt in a large bowl and mix well. Add the yeast and stir until dissolved. Add the shortening and mix well. Stir in 2 1/2 cups of the flour. Add enough of the remaining flour to make the dough easy to handle. Knead on a lightly floured surface until smooth and elastic. Shape the dough into 1-inch balls. Place three balls in each greased muffin cup. Let rise, covered, for 1 hour or until doubled in bulk. Bake at 400 degrees for 20 minutes.

Makes 1 1/2 dozen

Children are the bridge to heaven.

—Persian Proverb

Shrimp Bread

Seasoned Butter
1/2 cup parsley, finely chopped
3 large garlic cloves, minced
2 tablespoons finely chopped shallots
2 tablespoons blanched
    almonds, ground
1 tablespoon Pernod
1 1/2 teaspoons salt

1 teaspoon white pepper
1 cup (2 sticks) butter, softened

Bread
1 (14-inch) loaf French bread
1 1/4 pounds large shrimp, cooked
    and peeled
1/2 cup dry white wine

To prepare the butter, combine the parsley, garlic, shallots, almonds, Pernod, salt, white pepper and butter in a bowl and mix well.

To prepare the bread, cut the top from the bread and reserve. Hollow out the bread to form a shell, reserving the center pieces. Process the bread pieces in a food processor to form crumbs. Spread some of the seasoned butter in the bread shell. Layer with the shrimp, remaining seasoned butter and enough of the bread crumbs to fill the shell. Drizzle the wine over the top. Place the bread on a baking sheet lined with foil. Bake at 400 degrees for 15 minutes. Replace the reserved bread top. Bake for 10 minutes or until the bread is heated through and the butter melts. Cut into 12 slices. Serve hot, cold or reheated.

Serves 12

Man alone has the power to transform his thoughts into physical reality.
Man alone can dream and make his dreams come true.

—NAPOLEON HILL

Communion French Bread

1 long loaf French bread
1/2 cup (1 stick) butter, softened
1/4 cup red wine

1/2 cup (2 ounces) grated
Parmesan cheese

Cut the bread into thick slices, cutting to but not through the bottom. Whip the butter, wine and cheese in a bowl. Spread between the slices and over the top of the bread. Place on a baking sheet. Bake at 400 degrees for 10 minutes or until heated through.

Serves 6 to 8

Failure is only an opportunity to begin again more intelligently.

—HENRY FORD

Cheddar Cheese Spread with Port

1/4 cup port or sherry
2 tablespoons cream
1/4 teaspoon paprika

Dash of onion salt
8 ounces sharp Cheddar cheese,
cut into cubes

Process the port, cream, paprika, onion salt and cheese in a blender or food processor until smooth. Place in a serving bowl. Serve with assorted crackers. (*Note: The cheese spread can be molded by placing it in a small bowl and chilling it. Unmold onto a serving plate at serving time.*)

Makes 1 cup

As is our confidence, so is our capacity.

—WILLIAM HAZLITT

Ca C'est Bon Chili con Queso Dip

8 ounces ground round
1 tablespoon olive oil
2 large garlic cloves, pressed
1 large onion, chopped
2 (15-ounce) cans Mexican stewed tomatoes
2 tablespoons all-purpose flour
1/4 cup evaporated milk
2 to 3 (7-ounce) cans chopped green chiles
1/2 to 1 teaspoon chopped chile (optional)
1 pound Monterey Jack cheese, coarsely shredded

Brown the ground round in the olive oil in a skillet, stirring until crumbly. Drain the ground round, reserving enough of the pan drippings for sautéing. Add the garlic and onion to the reserved pan drippings. Sauté until the onion is translucent. Add the tomatoes. Simmer until the liquid is slightly reduced and the mixture is thickened, stirring frequently. Mix the flour and evaporated milk in a bowl to form a paste. Stir into the tomato mixture. Add the green chiles, chile and ground round and mix well. Stir in the cheese just before serving. Spoon into a chafing dish to keep warm. Serve with tortilla chips.

Serves 6 to 8

No legacy is so rich as honesty.
—WILLIAM SHAKESPEARE

Sensational Shrimp Guacamole

2 large ripe avocados, sliced
1 (4-ounce) can diced green chiles, drained
1 small yellow onion, finely chopped
1 garlic clove, minced
1 large tomato, coarsely chopped
2 tablespoons lemon juice
1 tablespoon extra-virgin olive oil
1 teaspoon salt
8 ounces cooked deveined shrimp, coarsely chopped

Combine the avocados, green chiles, onion, garlic, tomato, lemon juice, olive oil and salt in a bowl and mix well. Fold in the shrimp. Serve with tortilla chips.

Makes 2 cups

If you want the rainbow, you gotta put up with a little rain.

—DOLLY PARTON

Heavenly Hot Fudge Sauce

1 1/2 cups sugar
2/3 cup light corn syrup
1/4 cup (1/2 stick) butter

2 ounces unsweetened chocolate
1/2 cup heavy cream

Mix the sugar, corn syrup, butter and chocolate in a saucepan. Cook over low heat to 246 degrees on a candy thermometer, firm-ball stage, stirring constantly. Remove from the heat. Add the cream gradually, stirring constantly. Return to the heat. Cook for 5 minutes or to the desired thickness. Serve hot or cold.

Makes 2 cups

*We worry what a child will do tomorrow, yet we
forget that he is someone today.*

—STACIA TAUSCHER

T-Paul's Praline Sauce

1 1/2 cups packed dark brown sugar
2/3 cup light corn syrup
1/4 cup (1/2 stick) butter

1 cup evaporated milk
1 cup chopped pecans

Mix the brown sugar, corn syrup and butter in a saucepan. Cook over low to medium-low heat to 246 degrees on a candy thermometer, firm-ball stage. Remove from the heat. Stir in the evaporated milk. Return to the heat. Cook for 5 minutes or to the desired thickness. Stir in the pecans. Serve hot or cold.

Makes 2 cups

If you can dream it, you can do it.

—WALT DISNEY

Corn Relish

18 ears of corn
4 cups chopped cabbage (1 small head)
1 cup chopped green bell pepper
1/2 cup chopped red bell pepper
1 cup chopped onion
4 cups vinegar (1 quart)
1 cup water
1 1/2 cups sugar
1 tablespoon celery seeds
1 tablespoon salt
1 tablespoon turmeric
1 tablespoon dry mustard
1 tablespoon mustard seeds

Remove the husks and silk from the corn. Place the corn in a large stockpot and cover with water. Bring to a boil and boil for 5 minutes. Drain the corn and submerge immediately in cold water to stop the cooking process. Using a sharp knife, cut the kernels into a bowl; drain. Combine the drained corn, cabbage, bell peppers, onion, vinegar, water, sugar, celery seeds, salt, turmeric, dry mustard and mustard seeds in a large stockpot. Bring to a boil and reduce the heat. Simmer for 20 minutes. Pack into six hot sterilized 1-pint jars, leaving 1/2 inch headspace; seal with two-piece lids. Process in a boiling water bath for 15 minutes.

Makes 6 pints

Believe deep down in your heart that
you're destined to do great things.

—Joe Paterno

The Baron's Bayou-Style Boiled Peanuts

2 pounds raw peanuts
1/2 cup Creole seasoning
1/2 cup salt, or to taste
7 tablespoons liquid Cajun crab boil
41/2 quarts water

Soak the peanuts in water to cover in a large stockpot for 8 to 24 hours, weighing down with a large plate or lid to keep the peanuts fully submerged; drain and rinse.

Place the peanuts, Creole seasoning, salt, crab boil and 41/2 quarts water in a stockpot. Bring to a boil over high heat. Cover and reduce the heat to medium-low. Cook for 6 hours or until the peanuts are tender, adding additional water as needed to keep the peanuts covered and stirring occasionally. Remove from the heat. Let stand for 1 hour. Drain and store in the refrigerator. Enjoy the peanuts cold or reheat by microwaving, covered, on High for 3 to 5 minutes. These peanuts may also be used to make hummus, if you want a new twist on an old favorite. (*Note: For Traditional Southern Boiled Peanuts, omit the Creole seasoning and crab boil and use 2/3 cup salt instead of 1/2 cup.*)

Serves 14

*Fatherhood is pretending the present you love
the most is "soap-on-a-rope."*

—BILL COSBY

Hurricane "Rita" Sangria

1 bottle rioja wine
2 cups white cranberry juice
1/3 cup Cointreau
2 tablespoons grenadine
1 cup pomegranate juice
1 small orange, sliced
1 small apple, sliced
1 small pear, sliced
1 small lemon, sliced
3 whole cloves
2 cinnamon sticks

Combine the wine, cranberry juice, Cointreau, grenadine, pomegranate juice, orange slices, apple slices, pear slices, lemon slices, cloves and cinnamon in a pitcher and mix well. Chill for 2 hours. Discard the cloves and cinnamon before serving. Serve in ice-filled 8-ounce glasses.

Serves 12

Angels may not dress the part, with robes and wings that soar. Often angels come as friends, knocking at your door.

—ANONYMOUS

White Hot Chocolate

1/4 cup half-and-half or light cream
2/3 cup vanilla baking pieces or candy coating, chopped
1 (3-inch) cinnamon stick

1/8 teaspoon nutmeg
2 3/4 cups half-and-half or light cream
1 teaspoon vanilla extract
1/4 teaspoon almond extract

Combine 1/4 cup half-and-half, the vanilla baking pieces, cinnamon stick and nutmeg in a saucepan. Cook over low heat until melted, whisking constantly. Remove the cinnamon stick. Add 2 3/4 cups half-and-half. Cook until heated through, whisking constantly. Remove from the heat. Stir in the flavorings. Serve in mugs with candy canes.

Serves 5

I'm a slow walker, but I never walk back.

—ABRAHAM LINCOLN

The Big Easy Eggnog

6 eggs, separated
3/4 cup sugar
4 cups whole milk, scalded
1/4 teaspoon salt
1 (15-ounce) can evaporated milk

2 to 4 cups (about) brewed New Orleans-style chicory coffee or regular coffee (optional)
8 ounces brandy, or to taste

Beat the egg whites with one-half of the sugar in a mixing bowl until stiff. Beat the egg yolks and remaining sugar in a mixing bowl until thick. Mix the whole milk, salt and evaporated milk together; cool. Fold in the egg yolks and then the egg whites. Chill until serving time. To serve, mix 3/4 cup of the eggnog with 1/4 cup coffee and 1 ounce brandy per serving. Garnish with nutmeg. (Note: If you are concerned about using raw eggs, use eggs pasteurized in their shells, which are sold at some specialty food stores.)

Serves 8

The door of opportunity won't open unless you do some pushing.

—ANONYMOUS

Sparkling Strawberry Champagne

2 quarts strawberries
1/2 cup confectioners' sugar
2 liters Champagne, chilled

2 liters sparkling mineral
water, chilled

Purée the strawberries in a blender or food processor fitted with a steel chopping blade. Add the confectioners' sugar and process until dissolved. Strain through cheesecloth into a wide-mouth pitcher, discarding the solids. Chill until serving time.

To serve, pour the strawberry purée into a punch bowl over a molded block of whole strawberries in ice. Gently stir in the Champagne and sparkling water. Ladle into punch cups.

Makes 1 gallon

Every child born into the world is a new thought of God, an ever fresh and radiant possibility.

—KATE DOUGLAS WIGGIN

Lemon-Lime Wine Punch

3 (6-ounce) cans frozen limeade
concentrate, thawed
1 (12-ounce) can frozen lemonade
concentrate, thawed

1 (1 1/2-liter) jug cold dry white wine
(chablis or chenin blanc)

Fill a 1-quart ring mold with cooled boiled water. Freeze, covered, in the freezer. Blend the limeade concentrate, lemonade concentrate and wine in a punch bowl. Unmold the ice ring and add just before serving. Set out a bowl of lemon or lime wedges and a bowl of salt. Guests can rub their glasses with the lemon wedges and then dip the rim in salt before ladling in the punch.

Makes 3 quarts

A true friend is one who walks in when the rest of life walks out.

—ANONYMOUS

Brandy Milk Punch Iced Tea

2 quarts tea, chilled
1/2 fifth of brandy
3 pints vanilla ice cream
1 cup ginger ale
1/2 cup lemon juice

Process the tea, brandy, ice cream, ginger ale and lemon juice one-half at a time at medium speed in a blender, pouring into a pitcher after each batch. Serve over ice.

Serves 8 to 10

You cannot keep trouble from coming, but you needn't give it a chair to sit on.

—ANONYMOUS

RECIPE CONTRIBUTORS AND TESTERS

Thank you to all of the recipe contributors from OLQH School and the church community of Our Lady Queen of Heaven Catholic Church.

Contributors

Lisa Ange
Grant Armentor
Jane Baggett
Colleen Benoit
Nancy Best
Tricia Bertrand
Patsy Beverung
Lisa Bono
Brenda Borne
Staci Bruchhaus
Paula Bruce
Allison Burge
Angie Cain
Deacon George Carr
Sally Carrizales
Racheal Chiasson
Angie Chamberlain
Andrew Chehotski
David Chehotski
Natalie Comeaux
Anita Conrad
Erlene Conrad
Missy Conrad
Shannon Cox
Beth Crochet
Kim Crowe

Tracy Cunningham
Michelle Cutrera
Desiree Daigle
Madeline DeLucca
Denise Derouen
Brenda Desormeaux
Lori Duplechin
Mark Duplechin
Carrie Dondis
Ashley Eisen
David Falk
Julie Flaherty
Georgette Fontenot
Kelley Fontenot
Tonya Fontenot
Sheila Ford
Yolanda Fountain
Dionne Francois
Liz Fruge
Monsignor James Gaddy
Cassie Gage
Pam Goodwin
Tom and Susan Gorham
Tricia Guidry
Brandi Guillory
Rachael Guillory

Jodie Guth
Joni Hamilton
Vicki Hawsey
Gay Hebert
Tara Hebert
Ginny Henning
Susan Henning
Kristine Hilliard
Mrs. Warren M. Holmes
Leesa Howard
Debbie Hughes
CynDee Journey
Tracie Kadlubar
Bridget Kingery
Mary Kubiak
Rita LaBorde
Rita Landry
April Lee
Tammy Lewis
Kayla Little
Barbara Lorio
Annette Tritico-Manuel
Dawn Matte
Emmy May
Sherry May
Scott Meche

Lorena Mendez	Heather Sharpe	Cary Tassin
Jill Midkiff	Joan Sharpe	Dean Taylor
Merle Mouton	Joyce Simoneaux	Pauline Taylor
Michelle Mudd	Jared Smith	Christine Manuel-Vail
John Poerio	Vickie Smith	Marcy Wade
Jane Claire Radde	Lisa Sober	Yvette Ware
Anna Reyes	Britta Sole	Bridget Wharton
Linda Sartin	Terrye Stidham	Peggy White
Allison Savoy	Kim Stine	Marissa Whitebeck
Rachelle Schexneider	Jenny Sutton	Margaret Wright
Patty Scott	Colette Tanner	Kayla Young

Testers

Jane Baggett	Cassie Gage	Ramon O'Brien
Amber Belaire	Tricia Guidry	Linda Sartin
Colleen Benoit	Whitney Hanks	Patty Scott
Staci Bruchhaus	Ginny Henning	Heather Sharpe
Kim Conner	Susan Henning	Joyce Simoneaux
Anita Conrad	Mrs. Warren M. Holmes	Britta Sole
Erlene Conrad	Connie Houssiere	Jenny Sutton
Missy Conrad	Leesa Howard	Cary Tassin
Shannon Cox	Bridget Kingery	Jeannie Weise
Kim Crowe	Marie Loubet	Margaret Wright
Jennie Daley	Emmy May	
Madeline DeLucca	Sherry May	

INDEX

Creole for the Soul

To order *Creole for the Soul* cookbook and prints of the artwork,
contact OLQH School Office at:

3908 Creole Street
Lake Charles, Louisiana 70605
Phone: 337-477-7349 • Fax: 337-477-7384
ljakel@olqh.org

Cookbook price: $24.95, plus tax and shipping